ZEN COMES WEST

ZEN CONFERENCE

A snapshot taken by Miss Okamura in the Lounge of the Rembrandt Hotel, London, in June, 1958, of (L. to R.) Mr. Christmas Humphreys, Mr. Alan W. Watts and Dr. D. T. Suzuki.

Zen Comes West

THE PRESENT AND FUTURE OF
ZEN BUDDHISM IN BRITAIN

———

CHRISTMAS HUMPHREYS

Ruskin House

GEORGE ALLEN & UNWIN LTD
MUSEUM STREET LONDON

*Printed in Great Britain
in 11 on 12 pt. Imprint type
by East Midland Printing Company Limited
Bury St. Edmunds, Peterborough, Kettering
and elsewhere*

PREFACE

The purpose and scope of this book are sufficiently described in the Introduction. Chapters 1, 2, 8, 9 and 10 first appeared in *The Middle Way*, the organ of the Buddhist Society, London, and I am grateful to its Editor, Mrs Muriel Robins, for permission to reprint. For retyping the atrocious typing in which I 'write' my books I am grateful to many assistants, notably Miss Amy Bedwell, Mrs Mary Anthony and Miss Peggy Kennett. The Frontispiece is the only known photograph of the three persons most concerned in the subject of Zen comes West, Dr D. T. Suzuki, Alan Watts and myself. The snapshot was taken in the lounge of the Rembrandt Hotel, South Kensington in June 1958 by Miss Mihoko Okamura.

CONTENTS

CONTENTS

CONTENTS

13

INTRODUCTION

Zen Buddhism was founded by Bodhidharma in China in the 6th century A.D. and consolidated as a new School by the 6th Patriarch, Hui-neng, about two hundred years later. In due course this direct path to Enlightenment passed to Japan, where it is flourishing today. It first came West in 1927, with the publication of Dr D. T. Suzuki's first series of *Essays in Zen Buddhism*. Others of this great author's works appeared thereafter in rapid succession, and soon there was ample material for the study of this unique school of spiritual endeavour. In 1930 a Meditation Circle was founded in the Buddhist Society, and as time went on it became more and more interested in Zen.

In 1936 Dr Suzuki gave his famous talk at the opening meeting of the World Congress of Faiths, and visited the Society, and in the same year Alan Watts produced his *Spirit of Zen*, the first major attempt by a Westerner to write on the subject. But still there was no question of Zen training, still less of a Master being available to help us in our studies. We just felt the need to think more wholly, as a prelude to moving that much nearer to going beyond thought.

After the war there was a great expansion of interest in Buddhism, and when, on my return from the East in 1946, I was able to use a large sum given me by the Buddhists of Burma for the publication of hitherto unknown Buddhist texts, the stage was set for the sudden outburst of Zen which has been a feature of the last ten years in England. My own *Zen Buddhism* appeared in 1949, and Benoit's *The Supreme Doctrine* in 1951. Dr Suzuki, in 1953 and 1954, paid two visits to London, spending much time with the Zen Class at the Society. In 1953 appeared the English edition of Herrigel's *Zen in the Art of Archery*, the first description of Zen being practised, as it were, by a European. In 1957 W. J. Gabb, a member of the Society who had settled in South Africa, produced *The Goose is Out*. In 1958 Alan Watts returned to London after twenty years' absence, hard on the heels of his companion volume *The Way of Zen*, and during the summer Dr Suzuki spent much time with the Zen Class. He was impressed with the need of sending us the expert teacher which our efforts seemed to deserve. Professor Sohaku Ogata, who for thirty years sponsored and helped Western students to see something of Zen in Japan, came as the guest of the Society to its 1957 Summer School, and thereafter toured the Continent and refounded the Class on more formal Zen lines.

And still the books rolled out, Professor Ogata's *Zen for the West*, Robert Linssen's *Living Zen* and Wei-Wu-Wei's *Fingers Pointing Towards the Moon* all appearing in the spring of 1959. The interest is indeed growing and growing fast, and Dr Suzuki promised to do what he could on his return to Japan to find a Roshi, a qualified Zen Master, to give some substantial time to the needs of Europe. No such help has come, although our 'opposite number' in New York, the American Zen Institute, secured the services of the Ven. Miura for two visits of some months to help their Group in its studies. Of this Zen Institute Mrs Ruth Sasaki was one of the leading members, and it was her visit to England in the autumn of 1958 which drew our attention to the fact of the present crisis. Her views on the limits of Western work on Zen in the absence of a Master were clear, and the limits were narrow indeed. I summarised her views, and our own, in the *Middle Way*, the journal of the Buddhist Society for November, 1958, and received from a member in France the protest which launched the correspondence which appears as part of Chapter III.

So what should the Zen Class of the Society do? Candidates pour in and apply for admission to the Class. They are told that there is a Separate 'Beginners' Class' for those approaching Zen for the first time. Meanwhile the Zen Class bears a heavy responsibility. As the only organised group in Europe working on a system of training designed to lead towards Zen experience, it is the pioneer in a 'trackless waste'. For the question it has to face is no less than this—What can be done towards Zen experience in the absence of a trained teacher? That the need for Zen teaching in practice as well as theory is urgent and growing is now clear, and as the pioneer group we must bravely lead the way. But whither? What follows is material on which the reader may base his own reply.

After a brief chapter on Zen Buddhism and the components of the problem, I have given the views of Mrs Sasaki and my ensuing correspondence with a friend in France. So much for theory, but I have then given at some length the way in which the Zen Class works, partly in periodic letters to the Class from me, the incompetent but blindly courageous leader of the blind, partly in collations of notes of Talks to the Class, but for the most part in copy letters to members, whose names I have changed, about themes and problems and aspects of Zen teaching as they arise. Not all the letters are as written, as it simplified the compilation of the book to keep one theme to a letter, but the material is genuine. I have to a small extent graded them from simple to more advanced in theme or treatment, interpolating a section on *Concentration and Meditation* where it seemed to fit in.

I have then added three articles reprinted from *The Middle Way*, which are made up from the actual answers of the members to sets of questions given them to answer in writing. These are the members' attempts to express their own experience, as written for no one but myself to see. Hence the anonymity.

Finally, I have tried to summarise the situation to date and to estimate the affect of Zen study and practice on the Europe of tomorrow. The rest is for the reader.

Part One

ZEN COMES WEST

CHAPTER I

ZEN BUDDHISM

The School of Zen Buddhism may be viewed as part of the Mahayana school or entirely on its own. It uses all scriptures and is bound by none, and likewise uses any technique or means (*upaya*) which serves its end, which is to awaken the pupil's mind to its own enlightenment. But, whatever its genesis or place in the Buddhist field, it is unique in the long record of religious history. As a force it is responsible for the greatest art of China, and much of the finest culture of China and Japan. It has produced in those countries some of their greatest minds. Yet when describing Zen, and the history and technique of the school of Zen, it is easy to give a totally wrong impression, both of Zen and the school which seeks it. To regard it as 'fun and games', as witty nonsense or paradox gone mad, is to confuse the finger which points at the moon with the moon at which it points. These strange, provocative methods of speech and behaviour occur, it is true, in the course of transmission of Zen; they are not of its substance.

Yet the history of Zen may help to convey its nature and place in the Buddhist field. In India, where Buddhism was born, we find that not long after the Buddha's passing the exuberant Indian mind developed, from the original teaching, a magnificent range of brilliant and profound thought, and with it some of the world's greatest philosophers. This new philosophy went further East, and finally reached China. But the Chinese were not impressed with this wordy statement of Reality, and even more disliked the Sangha, because its members begged for food and did no work in the fields. The Chinese are a practical, earth-minded race, and believe that every man should work out his own salvation with diligence—in the fields.

This resistance was broken down in the 7th century A.D. by Bodhidharma, who was born of noble family in South India. He became one of the most advanced thinkers of his day, and in due course travelled to China. When he arrived, his reputation had preceded him, and he was invited to visit the Emperor of that day. The interview was most unusual. After the usual ceremony of the ancient Chinese Court, the Emperor began to boast of his many achievements for his people. He said:

'I have built many temples and monasteries, I have copied the sacred books. Now what is my merit?'

Bodhidharma replied: 'None whatever, Sire'.

The Emperor, taken aback, enquired:

'What is to be considered the first principle of the Dharma?'

Bodhidharma replied:

'Vast Emptiness and nothing holy therein.'

Asked the Emperor, not unreasonably:

'Who, then, is it who stands before me?'

'I have no idea' said Bodhidharma.

That, whether true or not, is an epigrammatic way of describing this tremendous teacher's original views on Buddhism, and Zen has been rightly described as China's reaction to Indian Buddhism. What in the Indian mind was best expressed in numerous volumes was, in China, compressed into a single sentence. Indian philosophy spoke at length of the Absolute. In China it was expressed thus: 'What', asked a pupil, 'is the One word of Reality'? Answer: 'You make it two'. The mode of expression, and hence of the transmission of experience, was in this way lifted from the plane of the intellect to the realm of super-consciousness which lies beyond concepts of any kind.

The ebullience of Indian thought was thus from the Zen point of view a decline from the spiritual heights at which the Buddha taught, and Chinese influence served to produce a reversion to its original, direct simplicity. Is Buddhism a school of thought erected about the teaching of the Buddha, or is it the record of His actual Enlightenment? The answer is obvious, that Buddhism is *Buddh-ism*, the 'ism' or school of *Buddh*, the Buddha's Awakening. All else now known as Buddhism has developed, with more or less excuse, from the one supreme experience which raised a man to Buddhahood. It follows that to drag from their grandiloquent heights the speculations of Indian philosophy was a move in the right direction. If so, the School of Zen is nearer than any other to the Light, and has the most right to be called the School of Buddha's Enlightenment.

What, then, is Zen? The answer is simple. It is the Buddha's Enlightenment, the Buddha's spiritual achievement attained as the guerdon of a thousand lives completely dedicated to that end. It follows that to know what is Buddhism, and therefore Zen, one must achieve the Buddha's experience. Anything less is less than Zen. The process of Enlightenment begins here, and now, with this, whatever is now in hand. The rest is a process of the mind's expansion until consciousness becomes commensurate at will with that which lies beyond imagining.

The Buddha was a man, not God, and his teaching was plain. 'This have I found—Suffering and the Way to the end of suffering. Where I have trodden all may tread. Work out your own salvation, with diligence'. That is reasonable. It is equally reasonable to speak of steps on the long path up the mountain to self-enlightenment. We are now on the valley floor. Perhaps we think that, having news of the summit, we are on the way. But are we? Are we even in training for the climb? If we go into training, learn the technique of climbing, study the way on maps (prepared by previous climbers), and develop the will to achieve success we shall at least be ready to climb. We know, for the Buddha has told us, what we shall find upon the way, but we shall not know the nature of the summit until we get there. But if we begin to climb, at least into the foothills, our vision will expand; we shall see more of the sunlight and more of the way. If we climb a little higher we shall see still more, but if we stay in our chairs and discuss the thoughts of others about the way, we shall stay, as most of us do stay, in our chairs. There is no lift up this mountain. Let us begin, then, to climb.

There are two ways of climbing; in a spiral, gently, by degrees; or fiercely, directly, straight. The first is the usual Buddhist way; the second, the 'sudden' way, is Zen. Bodhidharma is said to have laid down four propositions of Zen. 'A special transmission outside the Scriptures; no dependence upon words; direct pointing to the Mind of men; seeing into one's own nature and the attainment of Buddhahood.' That is clear enough, and is made the simpler by the maddening logic of Zen. If you want to climb a mountain, begin at the top.

But is this advice so strange to Western ears? Did not Jesus say, 'Seek ye *first* the Kingdom of Heaven, and all things shall be added unto you'? The journey, the change from this to that, is illusion. Only the Here is real and the Here is Now and This. The process lies in the mind, and the whole of circumstance is the field wherein to become aware of our own inherent bliss.

The approach to Zen is total, using the whole man. In the West we abide by logic, the instrument of the thinking mind. 'This being so, that is so; that being so, this follows'. In the East the approach is not in a straight line, of argument, but from every point of view at once, and each of them direct. Truth, to be utterly absorbed and known must be grasped by the whole man, using his instruments of sense, emotion, thought and intuition, and all other means which enable a man to grasp the Absolute. For Zen, like mysticism and pure philosophy, seeks the One but seeks it differently. 'The Many returns to the One. So be it, but to what does the One return?' What would the mystics say to that? Zen goes into the One and out of it, for Zen is the Many *and* the One, the living experience which transcends the distinctions of the mind. In terms of psychology, the Self which *knows* is born on the margin of the conscious and unconscious, and thereafter as it grows absorbs both equally. In terms of philosophy, the pilgrim treads a Middle Way between all extremes, but in Zen the straight and narrow way folds up to a point and the point is nowhere to be found. It is the centre of a circle whose circumference is everywhere, a circle whose centre is nowhere; it lives in the 'one thought-moment' beyond space and time. Always in life the moments that matter are where thought ends; they appear in nonsense, as lightning in sunlight, as a burst of laughter over a cup of tea. 'Usual life is very Tao', said a Master of Zen. But the usual life in which Zen shines is most unusual. It must be found if at all in daily life, or 'daily life' is out of the field of Zen, and Zen would not be Zen. For Zen is that which, in modern parlance, makes life tick, and will therefore appear in our daily chores as frequently and brightly as in meditation under a tree. It will not alone be found in peculiar robes or peculiar positions. And why? Because *satori*, the flash of enlightening, happens in the mind, and the mind is equally with us in the temple, the office and the lavatory. Only in our self-wrought circumstance will Zen appear, and even then when all distinction of holy and unholy, Zen and not-Zen is destroyed.

The process of finding it involves what Jung calls the withdrawal of projections. There must be no running away from life, still less from Zen. Yet men attempt to escape in many ways. They escape into pleasure, phantasy, superstition; into slothful inactivity, detective-stories, hobbies, dreams; into concepts that are a substitute for reality. They run away into illness, moodiness, insanity and death. Why? Because they fear the Reality they loudly claim to seek. Psychologists say that many of their patients' troubles arise from 'refused fear'. They know that they are afraid but fear to face the cause of it, the thing they fear. So they run from life while Zen delights in it, all parts of it, and laughs, not at it, for that implies duality, but with it as it sings and ripples and flows. It follows that in Zen it does not matter who or what we are; still less does it matter what we do, so long as we learn from the effects of what we do, which is in turn the consequence of what we are. How do we react to circumstance? With fear, or Zen?

The ways of approach to Zen are infinite; they are not confined to Japan, and there may be in time a Western school of Zen. The Japanese Rinzai school makes much use of the *koan*, a word or phrase which has no sense, no meaning. The most famous of all is 'mu', an absolute 'no' or 'not.' At this moment in Japan there are probably ten thousand *bonzes* or monks in fierce, unremitting concentration on some such *koan* as, 'Two hands make a sound of clapping. What is the sound of one?' The *mondo* is nearly as meaningless to our concept-ridden minds. It is a rapid question-answer, a kind of shorthand conversation between the pupil and the Master's highly trained and illumined mind, by which the pupil is helped to smash the limitations of thought, and to break through to the absolute point of view. The question may sound foolish, yet it is put in deadly earnest; the answer is always nonsense to the intellect. It may be a smile, a gesture, silence or a blow. If the pupil misses the point the Master tries again, and probably more violently. Anything, just anything is used and justified which raises the pupil's mind above duality, to the absolute awareness which transcends it. The limitation of all concept, which of its nature works by comparison, must be utterly broken before the pupil can genuinely say, 'I know'.

What, then, is Zen? Your answer is as good as mine, for there is none. The word is the Japanese corruption of the Sanskrit term

Dhyana, vaguely translated as meditation. Its meaning is the meaning of all life, for it is that which lies behind manifestation, and is therefore to us the Absolute. To know it while on earth is the supreme paradox and the supreme act of truth. None can reveal it, none conceal it. Asked by a pupil to reveal the essence of Buddhism, a Master replied by taking the pupil for a walk in the woods. They came to a bush of wild laurel in bloom. 'There', said the Master, 'You think I am concealing something from you. There is the essence of Buddhism'. Nor can a man see Zen or handle it. 'How when a man brings nothing with him?' asked a pupil. 'Throw it away', said the Master. 'What shall I throw when I am not burdened at all?' 'If so, bring it along'.

Zen lives in facts and hates abstractions. It therefore hates all concepts, as so many cages in which the flow of life is foolishly confined. Asked, what is Buddhism, a Master replied, 'I do not understand Buddhism'. Why should he? Is not the dawn and the singing of a bird, and the taste of tea and the touch of jade the direct experience of Reality? If not, what is? Zen is the flow of the river, and we on either bank shout loudly that the other is wrong. We cling to the banks who fear the flowing; we fear to live who fear to flow. Zen is in laughter and song and immediate acceptance. It refuses nothing, being all. It knows no good or evil for all is Good; nor ugliness where all is Beautiful. Above the dualities invented by men's minds is the absolute 'right' which in our hearts we know but which in our brains is clouded with opinion. He who accepts the moment finds the eternal moment, and in that Now all is and all is right. In the world of illusion we live by the laws and the moral codes of men; the mind of the Zen-illumined is free, not only of the bonds of love and hate and thinking but even of the notion that the mind is free. Such men have vision in their eyes, compassion in their every act. They know, and in their certainty show forth the heart's serenity. Not pausing to argue or define they just walk on unceasingly into error and out of it, uphill or down, and over a precipice if that is the forward way. When self is not, who suffers hurt from things? When hate and lust and illusion die in the mind from want of fuelling, what is there left but laughter and understanding, and a gentle walking on?

Zen, then, is in the here and now, and the right doing of this. It is to be found in the right posting of a letter or washing up. If not, it will not be found. Zen is the act of walking on, but there is no path, no walker and no goal. You say that this is nonsense. So it is, but it is super sense, an awareness shared by the poet, the lover and the child. And also by the self-enlightened man. The intellect is a brilliant tool, but when the river is crossed the raft is left behind. Thoughts should be servants. In the West they become our masters, and bind us on our sojourning. Asked by a pupil to set him free, the Master replied, 'Who puts you under restraint?' Was the Buddha's Enlightenment merely splendid thinking, or the act of reunion of the part with the whole, the conscious with the unconscious mind, that freedom when the self, in dying, learns that it is free? Asked 'What is Zen?' a Master replied, 'Walk on'.

CHAPTER II

ZEN COMES WEST

Western Buddhism stands at the cross-roads. In popular parlance it has reached the point of no-return. It has moved far from being one of a hundred alien and peculiar beliefs studied by a few enthusiasts, and become an integral part of Western thought. Some of its Schools are well established. Theravada study and practice is to be found in many of the European countries, the Prajnaparamita philosophy is being taken up under the lectures and writings of Dr Edward Conze, Tibetan ritual is active in parts of Europe, and now Zen has become so popular that it is in danger of becoming a cult.

From such a position it must needs go forward; the movement is now too deeply rooted to wither from want of attention or be killed by its inevitable foes. 'Western Buddhism' has passed from the condition of an idle phrase, and is becoming a visible fact. Whether there should be such a thing is beside the point; it is born and it is growing, and it means that the Buddhism of Europe will not be the Buddhism of Ceylon, or of China or Tibet, which are very different in form; nor will its Zen be entirely the Zen Buddhism of Japan.

But the Buddhism of the West will be still more different from that of the East than those of Ceylon and Tibet, for example, are from each other. The Eastern approach to Truth is, as Lily Abegg proves in *The Mind of East Asia*, total and intuitive; that of the West is analytic/synthetic and mainly intellectual. Its starting point is the vaunted 'scientific' approach to phenomena, whether objective

28

or in the mind. It moves from the particular to the general, from visible material to intellectual hypotheses; it believes in believing nothing until it must. It follows that a definitely Western Buddhism must in time emerge, and be none the less Buddhism for being Western. The same applies to Zen. The aim of Zen Buddhism is the direct approach to Non-Duality, and nothing less. All else is secondary, including morality, doctrine, and every kind of ritual. Zen Buddhism was born in China of Bodhidharma and Tao, with Indian Buddhism as its reincarnating 'source-material'. It passed to Japan, and is now associated with the culture which it built among that highly cultured people. Now the Japanese offer the West its history, its theory and doctrine, its practice in monasteries and in daily life, and its records of achievement.

These we have imported through the books of Dr D. T. Suzuki, whose name is all but coterminous with Zen as known and practised in the West. But we shall not import these goods and leave them permanently foreign, as Chinese restaurants, French fashions and American films. Rather we shall receive them, study them, test them, digest them, absorb their spirit and then reclothe them in our own idiom of thought and practice. Only in this way will they become the product and expression of our own minds, and thus a useful set of 'devices' to enable us to find and express 'our' Zen, that is, Zen as we shall find it.

Or shall we lose the thing we want in making Western clothes for it? Will Zen in the West be so intellectualised, not only in the approach to it but the thing when found, that it may be splendid but will not be Zen? The answer will depend on our power to achieve it for what it is, if not by Oriental technique then by something more appropriate, though we shall not lightly discard a method which has served the millions of the East for fifteen hundred years. It is true that Carl Jung and others have stressed the folly of the West attempting to import the spiritual technique of the East by the process of intellectual adoption, for in this way it is not grafted on to the individual unconscious so as to present a vital and natural growth. But as the great writer points out in the same volume,[1] in spiritual affairs 'everything depends on the man and little or nothing on the method', which is only 'the way laid down by the man that his action may be the true expression of his nature'.

[1] *The Secret of the Golden Flower*, p. 97.

If some in the West, therefore, find the Japanese technique a way which aptly expresses their own search for Reality, let them use it. Those dissatisfied can seek or create their own.

Meanwhile the Eastern and Western approach to the same goal is different, and the difference is well set out in two recent books on Zen,[1] the one by Dr Suzuki and the other by Alan Watts. But it is not fair to take Dr Suzuki's books as a sample of Eastern writing on Zen. He is unique and likely to remain so. There are other scholar-philosophers with a knowledge of Zen Buddhism; there are *roshis* in Japan who, writing nothing, have yet achieved a first-hand experience of Reality. Is there any other who, with the training of a philosopher, with enormous knowledge of Buddhism in Japanese, Chinese, Sanskrit and Pali, and a knowledge of Western thought in several languages, can yet say, with all the unclaimed authority of one who knows, what is Reality? For thirty years, from *Essays in Zen Buddhism, Series I*, in 1927 to this latest collection of essays in 1957, he has spoken to the world, both East and West, as far as any man in modern times has done so, from the plane of Prajna. Only from him can we take the logic of No-logic, and see that A is at the same time Not-A. He truly is a living bridge from the Absolute to the Relative, a leader from the Unreal to the Real that dwells in the Unreal, and those still locked in the cage of concept, who cannot see him so, are to be pitied for their chains.

Who else presents the Japanese way of Zen? Professor Sohaku Ogata has written *Zen for the West* on the strength of two years' work in the USA and three months in Europe. But for him Dr Suzuki is the Master, one whose very presence takes one further on the way, and he would not claim to stand beside him. Yet, these Eastern teachers alike criticise the West for being too intellectual. Herrigel alone, they seem to say, in his *Zen in the Art of Archery* has caught the spirit of Zen, but then he learnt it from a Master of Zen in Japan. This rules out my own *Zen Buddhism*, Benoit's *The Supreme Doctrine*, and Robert Linssen's *Living Zen*. It also rules out Alan Watts' *Spirit of Zen* and his new book, his *magnum opus* on the subject, *The Way of Zen*. Can nobody, then, write usefully on Zen who has not studied long in a Zen monastery? No words

[1] *Mysticism, Christian and Buddhist*, Allen & Unwin, 1957.
   The Way of Zen, Thames and Hudson, 1958.

can express the discovery of Zen, but even a Japanese *roshi* uses them, and if the West is more thoughtfully than intuitively inclined we must find a technique which begins with thought and then by finer and finer thought transcends it. Clearly the intuition is needed to achieve Prajna, and Western minds are paralysed by a system of education which does not recognise its existence. Very well, then, we must examine and develop this faculty of direct cognition, and then use it to attain what thought can never know.

In the very first chapter of *Mysticism, Christian and Buddhist*, Dr Suzuki sets out what he has long disclosed in many of his works, his enthusiastic adoption of Eckhart as not only the greatest of Western mystics but one who in his own terminology was talking Zen. He quotes Ananda Coomaraswamy, a fellow enthusiast, on Eckhart's 'astonishingly close parallel to Indian modes of thought', not by borrowing but because of 'the coherence of the metaphysical tradition in the world at all times'. Eckhart knew the distinction of the Godhead from God, of the indescribable Absolute and its first manifestations. He even described, as Dr Suzuki frequently describes, why God created the Universe, that He might know Himself. If Eckhart, a German, can so find, cannot we too? True, Eckhart left no pupils, but then Zen Buddhism is unique in this, that it is the sole School in which such mystical experience is not only taught, but the way to it is taught, and pupils are trained in turn to teach.

And Buddhist philosophy is again unique in that it is based on the Buddha's personal experience. 'Whatever knowledge the philosopher may have, it must come out of his experience', which is 'seeing', seeing things in their state of suchness or 'isness', a term which Eckhart himself employs. In brief, 'personal experience is the foundation of Buddhist philosophy, and the function of the intellect consists in leading the mind to a higher field of consciousness by proposing questions which are beyond itself'. Thus we in the West must ask and ask, that we may learn that the intellect alone will not answer. For 'Zen's first concern is about its experience and not its modes of expression'. These are of the field of action in which the West excels, yet so in a way is experience, for *satori* is not an abstract idea but a concrete fact, as lightning is a concrete fact.

What 'self' acquires it? St Paul spoke of body, soul and spirit.

31

We know the body; 'soul' and 'spirit' are fundamentally two, though one. And Dr Suzuki, in a single paragraph, sweeps aside the tedium of the Theravada's views on self, re-unites the Dharma with the Indian source from which it emerged, and raises the eyes of the individual part to the Whole which is infinite. After speaking of the *gahakarika*, the 'builder of the house' of self from which, being free, the newly enlightened one knows that he is free, he says: 'The *gahakarika* is our relative empirical ego, and the mind freed from its binding conditions (*sankhara*) is the absolute ego, Atman, as it is elucidated in the Nirvana Sutra. The denial of Atman as maintained by earlier Buddhists refers to Atman as the relative ego and not to the absolute ego, the ego after enlightenment-experience. Enlightenment is seeing the absolute ego as reflected in the relative ego and acting through it'. (p. 47). Here is the world of our own experience, of a better and worse self, of the one that must be slain that the other may know itself as it is, 'self-identified' or 'inter-diffused' with the All and with the Absolute.

There is nothing here to negative my thesis, that though the early stages on the journey may be harder for Westerners than for their Eastern brothers on the Way, it is one way to one end, to be found not in a heaven which is elsewhere, but in the 'one moment' which is here and now and doing this. How then, does Alan Watts' new book assist his fellow-Westerners to achieve the same 'experience'? He does not claim to have studied in Japan, nor to have had any training under a *roshi* in the USA, but he still has the brilliant mind which gave us *The Spirit of Zen* at the age of nineteen, and he has learnt enough Chinese to read originals for himself.

With this equipment, being dissatisfied with any existing book on the subject, in that none gives what is to him essential, the Taoist and Indian background, he sets out to supply the deficiency. In his Preface he says, 'I am not in favour of "importing" Zen from the Far East, for it has become deeply involved with cultural institutions which are foreign to us. But there are things which we can learn, or unlearn, from it and apply in our own way'. So far we agree, but I do not see the need for his suggested third position between the 'objective' observer of Zen who, as he brightly points out, eats the menu instead of the dinner, and the 'subjective' disciple who does not know what dinner is being eaten. As he himself says, 'To know what Zen is, and especially what it is not, there is no alternative but to practise it, to experiment with it in the concrete so as to discover the meaning which underlies the words'. But this can only be done from 'inside' with the full enthusiasm of a mind bent to that end. When he wishes to add some measure of the objective Western viewpoint I am with him, and would refer to the second step of my own suggested Western approach to Zen, but there is no need for the 'friendly neutral position' he proposes. (As the Master Ummon said, 'If you walk just walk. If you sit, just sit. But don't wobble'). There need be no fear of our entanglement in the 'institutions' of Zen Buddhism, unless the fear is of becoming impaled on the finger instead of looking at the moon. But if the West, in its practice of Zen, is prepared to create its own institutions the trouble will not arise.

To sum up—if I can—my yet uncertain thoughts on a vast and urgent subject, the West needs Zen and Japan has it. But the West must have Zen without its Japanese clothing as soon as Western clothing can be made for it. But the clothing is unimportant compared with the achievement of the experience. How to attain the experience without a visit to Japan? The answer is—by study of the background of Buddhism and the history of Zen, by meditation, regular and deep, by the deliberate cultivation, by all 'devices' possible, of the power of the intuition, and by having in Europe from time to time such help from Japan as we need, until our own *roshis* have emerged and been given the 'seal of transmission', that they in turn may train their pupils to that same high office and responsibility.

The problem is urgent, and yet unsolved. What do our readers say?

CHAPTER III

THE PROBLEM BECOMES ACUTE

In the August issue of the *Middle Way* we included a brief note of the great honour done by the Zen Buddhists of Japan to Mrs Ruth Sasaki, the widow of the Japanese Roshi, Sokei-an Sasaki, around whose teaching to a group of students in New York the First Zen Institute of America was built up. In October Mrs Sasaki paid an all too brief visit to London and of course visited the Zen Class at the Society's headquarters. There she was pressed for her views on 'Zen for the West', and it was clear that some of these did not accord with our own. I recorded the visit in a brief article in the November issue in which, after referring to the foundation of the First Zen Institute, I continued, 'This was the pioneer group of Westerners to study and attempt to practise Zen in self-preparation for the coming of a qualified Roshi from Japan. Their efforts were rewarded by two visits from Miura Roshi who, however, has now once more returned to Japan. Then Mrs Sasaki, after years of negotiation and preparation, persuaded the governing body of Daitoku-ji, one of the largest Rinzai Zen monasteries in Kyoto, to rebuild a very old but ruined sub-temple in its enormous grounds, and to use it as a training school for Western students of Zen. As a climax, Mrs Sasaki was honoured as no Westerner has ever been honoured before, by making her not only a member of the Order, but a 'Head Priest' or 'Chief Monk' of the newly rebuilt sub-temple, and as such ranking with the others of that title throughout the monastery. On her way from Japan to New York for a visit Mrs Sasaki called in at London and spent much of her short five days with members of the Society. She attended a meeting of the Zen class and a tea and dinner party at our home, and had talks with members of all persuasion in the field of Buddhism. She has enormous knowledge of present day Japanese Buddhism, and in particular of the origin, history and present position of Rinzai Zen. All that she has to say, therefore is well worth considering carefully, though opinions may rightly differ as to the applicability of what she says to our special conditions here. For myself, I made the following notes after her departure, though others may not agree with my understanding of what she said or its interpretation.

For Mrs Sasaki, Zen is the product of an historical Zen tradition, and has no meaning outside that context. The sole way to achieve the Zen experience is by long training at the feet of qualified Zen masters. At present this means in Japan and in the Japanese language. No one should attempt Zen work who is not emotionally and intellectually well balanced, for the strain is considerable. No one should attempt *koan* practice without a master. The basis of Zen progress is a sound understanding of the origin and history of the school, of Buddhist principles in general and Zen scriptures in particular, and a most careful study of the very specialised and technical terms used.

So far I for one agree. But Mrs Sasaki further holds that the beginning of Zen meditation should be counting the breaths, if need be for years, and that save for the study of recognised master's sermons or sayings, this is all that Western students, in the absence of a Roshi, can usefully do together. Discussion, in her view, is worse than a waste of time. Here I respectfully disagree. I find that the minor Zen experiences do come as the result of such discussion, kept so far as possible at intuitive level, while mere sitting and counting the breaths can itself become a cage for the mind which must learn to 'abide nowhere'. But for some time at least it is an excellent practice, and the best for all beginners. So we shall carry on in our way, and leave our American friends to continue with theirs. Meanwhile we are deeply grateful for Mrs Sasaki's stimulating presence and advice.

One result of this expression of my views in the *Middle Way* was a fiercely worded protest from a subscriber who is an old friend of my generation, an Irishman living in France, and our correspondence was carried on through the winter of 1958-9. In his opening letter the reference to p. 106 of the *Middle Way* is to the words 'So far I for one agree', referred to in the preceding paragraph.

November 9, 1958.

Dear Toby,

Does anybody ever render you the service of holding up a mirror so that you may see a reflection of your verbal visage when it appears to be having a pain?

The first six words of the last paragraph on p. 106 of the current issue of the *Middle Way* will serve as a text. Therein you categorically accept what appears to be one of the most fantastic statements ever made on the subject of Zen.

What Mrs Sasaki describes is surely the exact opposite and contradiction of the Buddhist principles in general and Zen scriptures in particular on which her views are based?

I am not going to write you an essay. You presumably know these principles and scriptures much better than I. Without re-reading all Suzuki, enough are to be found in Alan Watts' chapter on the Rise and Development of Zen, or in Hui Neng or in Huang Po. What Mrs Sasaki conceives to be Zen appears to be a purely disciplinary technique, condemned by all the enlightened masters who spoke from a state of satori, a manipulation of the psyche, on a par with the process, attributed to some Tibetans, of boring a hole in the forehead with a bit-and-brace, or the ingerence of mescalin.

Not only is all this in direct contradiction with the plain words of these masters, it is equally in contradiction with an understanding of what they sought to convey, whether that understanding be merely intellectual or intuitional. Their teaching was rooted in Taoism and Mahayana Buddhism, on the spiritual plane of those teachings, and of the same spiritual stature as Vedanta Advaita. What would Huang Po, Hui Neng or the Maharshi have thought about such a technique for the abolition of the false identification and the realisation of the real nature?

What Zen may have become in modern Japan you know better than I, but we all know what has become of the doctrine of Jesus and of the doctrine of Lao Tzu. No doubt all the religions have had a similar experience. But, if that is so, it is also a fact that the pure doctrine has survived and is still available and practised, if only by a few. You surely understand the pure doctrine: it is simple enough and clear enough, and its truth is obvious enough, even if our burden of ignorance is still too heavy to allow us to break through completely and finally. Is it not the business of those who are in that position to urge these who are not yet—to keep their eye on the ball?

To me, if Zen means anything it means, as the masters said again and again in their vague Chinese, that Mind Itself cannot be sought by a manipulation of what is merely a false identification . . .

November 24, 1958.

Dear Terence,

In spite of the withering violence of your letter of the 9th, I still hold to the same opinion. It would take a longer letter than I have time for, for me to give my reasons, but in brief, they are these: Satori is the result of a specific process of breaking through the bonds of conceptualism and its consequent duality. To this end a school with traditions and technique has been built up over 1500 years and produced a large number of persons who have achieved that experience. True, in the early days, Masters taught their pupils without any particular technique, and only as spontaneous inspiration waned did the *koan* and *mondo* technique begin to take its place. Now we in the West become interested in Zen. We have no tradition, no school, no technique. What is worse, we have no Masters, we do not know when we are aiming in the right direction, and if, in great effort, we aim in the wrong direction, we may shatter the mind. We therefore humbly look to those who in 1500 years have built up this technique, and I am impressed with Ruth Sasaki's experience which covers, mark you, 20 years of working among Westerners and many years working in a Zen Monastery. Suzuki said more or less the same thing and, indeed, his comment to Alan Watts in my presence was to the effect 'You have written and talked about Zen for a long time; why not come to Japan and find it?' Certainly, we have found that we learnt more and advanced further in a few days round the feet of a Master than in months and years of working on our own. We could no more find it for ourselves than a child in the first form of mathematics could split the atom. Either we import the Masters to teach us via the technique or we go where the Masters live.

37

In theory, any one of us can find Zen any day. In practice, we don't, and to the extent that we do get genuine 'experience' it is by the study of Suzuki's books, strenuous mental self-discipline and much meditation in one way or another. Everything about the Zen tradition helps to this end, even its history. To imagine that we can do without it is, to me, arrogance. In the result, my own Zen Group have attained in the last few years results comparable with the extent to which we attempted to tread in the footsteps of this tradition and technique. It is painfully easy to know a lot *about* Zen. We learn this from books and write accordingly, but I gather that the Zen pundits in Japan regard only two Westerners as having got anywhere yet in Zen. One was Herrigel, who spent years in Japan under a Master, and the other is Ruth Sasaki, of whom the same applies.

I therefore cling to my opinion that Western students can only 'work out their own salvation with diligence' by humbly building on the experience of the East. Only thus can a Western tradition be founded and a Western technique built up. Only thus can our minds approach No Mind; but if *you* have found some other way of progress, we long to know of it. We are trying to learn. Meanwhile, waiting humbly and ferociously for the answer,

I am,

Yours sincerely,

November 27, 1958.

Dear Toby,

I much appreciate your kind letter and lucid explanation, but I am distressed that my letter appeared to be witheringly violent. Re-reading the carbon I see that it could appear so, but that is the effect of my lamentable style which seeks concision at the expense of normal emphasis—and the recipient cannot see the smile on the face of the tiger!

I am wondering if we sufficiently realise that nations who think they hold a monopoly of a traditional doctrine always tend to regard other nations who interest themselves in those doctrines with any degree of independence as heretics and worse? People who have lived in Japan have told me that in this respect the Japs are abnormally sensitive, in all departments of life. Do they like us daring to think for ourselves? Shall we ever get anywhere if we don't? Herrigel, yes, he is the only one they like (as far as I know), but, as you say, he did it under their tuition. And did he do anything but learn to use his organic consciousness? Was that the Complete and Perfect Enlightenment of the Buddha?

Are we not facing up to a complete and radical split? On the one hand the doctrine of Lao Tse, elaborated by Chuang Tse, married to that of the Buddha—or to what is attributed to him— in the Diamond Sutra and the Lanka, elaborated by the Patriarchs and their successors down to and including Rinzai, together with the Upanishads, Advaita Vedanta in general, down to Maharshi and Atmananda today; and, on the other, the systems and disciplinary techniques, manipulations of the psyche, of which the most important is modern Japanese Zen—all so categorically condemned by the former? Is that not now happening under our eyes, even under our hands? It is a situation to be understood.

You ask me if I have found some other way of progress, and that you long to know of it. Of course I have. What else am I doing? And it appears to be quite new. Some longish time ago I had an intuition. I was struck by the apparent fact that nobody I knew or read appeared to believe what those who were unquestionably awakened had told them—from the Buddha himself down to the Maharshi; or, alternatively, if they believed it, they spoke, wrote and acted as though they did not—which meant that they thought like that and did not, in fact, understand. So I started re-reading all the sages on the supposition that they really meant what they said, and that I had to understand it at all costs. It was quite long and arduous, but I was greatly helped by penetrating modern minds, much better than my own, which is synthetic, such as Benoit, John Levy, Alan Watts (to mention some that you will know), and their penetration helped me even when I could not feel that they themselves had understood what they had explained to me. (I should have added the learned Prof. Evans-Wentz to my list above).

Now I am faced with the job of trying to tell you what these statements of the masters are, that nobody appears to take literally or really understand, and which describe the barrier between us and awakening to reality, and the job of doing that without pages of quotation and disquisition. But ultimately, perhaps, there is only one, for the others really follow from it if we have understood. So I will quote the Diamond Sutra; all the awakened have said it, each in his own words, but those attributed to the Buddha are as clear as any. Again and again he tells us that the barrier is 'cherishing the *idea* of an ego-entity, a personality, a being, or a separated individuality.' An omnibus edition that leaves no loop-hole—or so one would have thought!

In Section VI, after saying that, as often elsewhere, he goes on to say, 'They will neither fall back to cherishing the *idea* of things as having intrinsic qualities, or even of things as devoid of intrinsic qualities. Wherefore? Because if such men allowed their minds to *grasp* and *hold on to* anything they would be cherishing the *idea* of an ego-entity, a personality, a being, or a separated individuality . . . '

In Section XXII: 'Through the Consummation of Incomparable Enlightenment I acquired not even the least thing.'

We have all read that a dozen times? We have, but have we believed it?

People who answered questions in plainer language, such as Huang Po and the Maharshi, said the same thing, more in our own way of speaking. We have read that also, but have we believed it?

The reason we have not is surely that we have not been able to see how it not only can but must be so. And some of those who have seen that have, nevertheless, not been able to believe what they themselves have demonstrated. So strong is the resistance.

I can only point a finger by asking, 'How could an object of consciousness (and the ego-notion is nothing but that) be also a conscious object?'

'What could there be to *grasp*, and who is there to grasp anything? Satori, Nirvana, is not in time—and therefore cannot be an *experience*. And how could an object of consciousness "grasp" anything outside time?' But does anybody, any school or sect do anything but strive and grasp, chasing their shadows, by every means they can hear of or devise?

Discoursing is not in my line; I can only point towards what I see. The I-notion cannot seize reality, but reality can enter and enlighten those objects of consciousness called Toby and Terence if they are in a state to receive us (not 'it' but 'us', for we are reality and nothing else whatever.) We have only to find that objects are empty.

Yours,

December 15, 1958.

Dear Terence,

Many thanks for yours of the 27th November. I think the trouble between you and me is always that you are too far into the world of theory and doctrine and maybe I am too far into the world of daily practice. I have found it too easy to tell myself and the others what should be done, and terribly hard to tell myself and others how to do it. I entirely agree with you in theory that the teachings of all the Masters agree that the enemy of all Enlightenment is self in the sense of an idea of a separate individuality. This is the great heresy of self as described in *The Voice of the Silence*, but assuming we believe this to be true, what do we *do*, literally, day by day to turn this belief into useful action, in the sense that a man believes a thing when he behaves as if it were true? What I do in my Class may be laughable; logically, philosophically and in terms of all theory. But I find that it works and seems to be psychologically sound. Students come to me for private interviews to say what they might not like to say in open class, and though in some sense the thirty of them are treading thirty different paths to the same end, still they are all progressing, and nothing that anybody says to me will persuade me that that is not true. It is far too easy to say that there is no self, or goal, that there is no progress on any path. The answer is that there is, and day by day these people are becoming more integrated, serene, able to cope with crises, large and small, more 'mindful and self-possessed', and through the lessening of the sense of self, more consciously compassionate and aware of all else that lives.

Does this help our attempt to understand each other? If it seems to be rude, it is not meant so. With all good wishes,

Yours ever,

December 18, 1958.

Dear Toby,

I am delighted to have your reply, and I thank you sincerely. It is just because I too am so anxious that we shall understand one another that I write, knowing what a burden a further job of work must be for you. But my anxiety extends to all of us—for I see gulfs widening; between English and continental Zen, and between Buddhism and Advaita. And it may be because to me there is no doctrine but only an explanation that the differences between them make no impression whatever.

One of the outstanding points in your letter is the query— assuming that we believe that no self exists, what do we do to turn this belief into useful action in the sense that when a man believes he behaves accordingly. The answer surely is that believing is not enough, not nearly: he must *know* it. When he knows it the re-adjustment will occur all by itself.

I most heartily congratulate you on your success with your pupils; please don't think that I underrate it. But I may not take it quite at its face value. Why? Because I cannot avoid asking whether you may not be perfecting the hansom cab? May you not be doing what the saints did, rather than what the sages did? May you not be trying to reach the results of the sages by the methods of the saints? Are you sure you are not just working on what has been called the organic consciousness, in a positive sense only, the organic con-sciousness being the engine-driver, and perhaps the engineer, of our relative reality?

It is difficult to believe in daily practice, because after all WHO practices? and WHO is progressing in each of your 30 prospective saints (or sages)? Who is there to 'progress' except the *reality* of each? Can that progress? Is it not all in the sphere of relativity? But is not the object to transcend relativity rather than to achieve anything therein? Huang Po thought it sufficiently important to say many times 'for you cannot use the mind to seek something from mind, nor the Buddha to seek something from the Buddha' (14). Are you not feeding the vampire rather than realizing that he isn't there—which would be enough? Satori, not being in time, can hardly be an experience.

Do you not think that though many of us understand that what we see as the perceptible universe is only an interpretation of chemical changes in a retina transferred by nerve-impulses to cause chemical changes in brain-matter, and can bear no recognisable relation to non-temporal, non-spacial, non-dual reality which is the suchness of everything we perceive, comparatively few realize that we ourselves are such objects of consciousness (I mean of course that 'we' that we are used to thinking ourselves), that the we who understand, or do not understand that are ourselves part of that dream—except in so far as we are reality? Just as we must be everything in our sleeping dreams, since it is we who dream them, so must we be everything in our waking dream, since we are reality. We are every object of consciousness, but in their suchness not in their appearance, not single objects of consciousness, separate and conceiving other objects. To believe in our existence as such is simply impossible!

The greatest discovery possible to man is the *knowledge* that there is no 'I' but I. No comparable thrill is imaginable! But until it is *experienced* the illusion holds full sway. Then even gravity is no more.

Let's all have sympathy for what we are all doing!

Yours,

February 8, 1959.

Dear Terence,

It is a long time since I got yours of the 18th December, but much has happened since. However, our correspondence seemed to me so valuable, as expressing points of view, both right and both limited, that I took the liberty of reading some of both our letters to our Group, to await their comment. It was most interesting and, as I expected, at the end of an hour they at least approached the middle.

Surely your distinction between saints and sages is 'falsely imagined'? I agree with Benoit that no preparation takes one to the goal, no morality produces enlightenment, and no intellectual understanding produces satori. But how did you get to your present awareness, from the protoplasmic slime of our material ancestors to the first-class intellect with which you were born? The answer is by growth, which involved effort, and at some time planned effort. The growing understanding, of 'who practises' is itself a growth of understanding, and unless the results of my students' efforts were to decrease the sense of self, and to increase the intuitive moments in depth and frequency, then were our labours barren indeed.

We are studying Mahayana philosophy—the Prajnaparamita—

43

with Dr Jaini, a brilliant young Indian, and our present subject is precisely what you so well describe, the illusion of the ego. But we must hear it, learn it, understand it, before we experience it—*pace* all the Benoits in existence; then wait for the actual experience.

I know that in Zen language you are right—*begin* with the satoric experience that there is no I, then see how to get the experience, and I have even done this running up one of the Malvern Hills. But still, in cold practice we jump, if it is a jump, from the bottom to the top, and must we not practise jumping?

Yours aye,

February 10, 1959.

Dear Toby,

You speak of what I am doing. Well, without abandoning the Master I have gone off on my own. I realise more and more that they answered questions posed by people of another race, another age, and another cultural background, and I doubt whether all the translators have understood what they were saying, either intellectually or intuitively. Do you not agree that we must re-express these things in our own idiom, not via translation but from our own understanding?

Yes, what we do undoubtedly involves effort, but effort for the work's sake, not for the result of the work (yes, yes, the Gita: I remember). We must seek no reward, either.

I don't see how either saints or sages, as long as they operate via themselves in a false identification, can ever get anywhere that matters much. But when they operate as I-reality I'd expect both of them to reach home together.

Terence.

In a letter of April 3, 1959, I spoke of other matters and then of my attempt to record, in this present book, the work of the Zen Class for a wider audience, 'by way of trying to help.'

April 4, 1959.

Dear Toby,

Your letters always stimulate me to comment, and to share the comment on the chance that something therein might happen to be worth sharing.

I know of no way in which one can help anybody, nor believe that there is any, other than the very limited one of trying to answer direct questions or supplying the answers in written form in case anyone should happen on the one needed. But I am willing to believe that the awakened may—as it is said—be able to do something of the kind in their grace-ful silence. Certainly not by talking or lecturing or discoursing unasked.

It might interest you to hear that of five people, four of whom I know pretty well, four of whom among those who appear to have penetrated furthest, three very well-known, *all* are now seriously ill in mind or/and in body, as a result—so I believe and as four of them know—of frustration, of realizing that all their understanding has led them nowhere and is of no help in their trouble. Yes, pretty startling, isn't it? One cannot but look for the reason. Of course, I don't know it, but I can give you my guess. They have understood 'everything' but the essential, i.e. that the ego must only be regarded as a working hypothesis; really to be rid of the notion would be the complete and supreme enlightenment of the Buddha, but its non-existence can be clearly comprehended even though it has to be utilised as a formula in daily life.

That is a kind of answer to your denial that first one must understand that. First, no, of course not—for it is the most difficult of all things (presumably) to grasp. People neither can, nor will face it. Like the apparent world being just a concept in consciousness. So—not first in the time sequence, but first in the sense of until that—nothing.

Best of good wishes for your interesting letters; they should help a few people, if anything can.

Yours very sincerely,

45

Part Two

CLASS WORK

CHAPTER IV

PREPARATION FOR THE JOURNEY

Dear Mr Brampton,

You say that you want Zen, and want instructions where to find it. But you have it. As the Egyptian Hierophants said long ago, 'The Light is within thee—let the Light shine!' This is not mere mystical jargon, but profoundly true. There is indeed no search for Zen— only the removing of the obstacles which prevent our normal consciousness being aware of our Enlightenment. In your case the worst obstacle is thought. You say that now you have retired you will have time to 'think things out.' This is an admirable pro- gramme, to help you find what you are, what you want, and what you propose to do with your leisure. To get your philosophic bearings, so to speak, to know what you know and believe, and certainly don't believe, all this is excellent, and far preferable to the usual round of golf, library books, gossip and beer. But all this is only the preparation for the approach to Zen, not even the prepara- tion *for* it, much less a near approach. I agree that it is necessary to get things straight, and to think clearly before beginning the journey beyond thought. But you cannot appreciate too soon that none of this 'planned thinking' brings you even within measurable distance of the practice of Zen. Zen is not a new hobby, an added factor in a life of leisure. It is *actual awareness* of the Absolute-Everything- All. Is *this* what you want? Then you must pay for it!

In life there is nothing, nothing whatever worth having for which

D   49

we do not have to pay. Even at a free lecture you pay with your time, 'bus fare and intelligent interest. What are you prepared to pay for what some call Zen? I will tell you some things which you must hand over, which I too am in process of surrendering. You must surrender the fetters of knowledge and thought. Not the knowledge, for it can be useful, and some is necessary. Nor thinking, for the human beings who are greatest spiritually have all had, it would seem, tremendous minds. But being bound to knowledge, principles, conclusions, ideas and even beliefs and opinions, that is what puts us under restraint. It is not merely admitting that the other fellow may be right, but realising that *you* must be, at least partially, wrong. Why? Because all knowledge in the field of relativity, and all knowledge *is*, is partial, limited, and therefore from the ultimate stand-point wrong. Nor is it enough to wish to be free from such fetters. You have read of the pupil who asked the master, 'Master, what shall I do to be free?' And the master answered, 'Who puts you under restraint?' These are your fetters tied on by you. *You* must undo them.

Then you must surrender all that you, Mr Brampton, have acquired from life, of honour and prestige, your O.B.E., your car and your fine collection of prints of old London. Not that you need give them away or sell them, or learn to despise them. But what would you be if you found yourself tomorrow morning disgraced, alone and penniless? Where would Mr Brampton stand then? You must therefore drop all grasping, including the holding to what you have, and that which you would become, perhaps captain of your golf club, or with a seat on the Borough Council. We need to let go what we have, not to add to ourselves, whether in the process we 'grow' in the public eye or 'become as nothing in the eyes of men', as the occult saying has it.

At present you move, to the eye of the man of Zen, on the tram-lines of a heavy, typically western, logical progression of thought and associated values. This is right, that wrong, this is to be acquired (with courtesy and fair play), that not. But if only you could suddenly see behind yourself I can assure you that the imp of Zen is rocking with laughter, and not kindly and with you, but at you. Can you lift yourself from the tramlines, soar on the wings of poetry, sink into the arms of glorious music, play the fool?

Let me give you a new idea. Play with it and let it play with you.

Zen is non-duality, not this or that or any thing or power or faculty. It *is*, and man and the universe are but two of its million million fleeting forms. Don't confuse non-duality with oneness. The One is a concept, for it can be conceived. Non-duality cannot, for it lies beyond the many and the one. It is not one, not two, not both and not neither. You can't get hold of it. *Don't try.* For while the part sees the Whole there is no Zen, for there are still two things, the part and the Whole. Zen awareness must be an expansion of consciousness beyond all knowledge of any kind and beyond all process. It must include the unconscious in this consciousness. There must therefore be a change of centre from the present ego-centredness of 'I' to a new centre, beyond or other than the conscious and unconscious. This is not my theory, for Jung says it and Suzuki says it, in different terms but without reference to each other. This only is the true Self, the babe that shall grow and become the universe. *Now* do you see that so long as the part is partial there can be no Zen? But when the part is let go, and allowed to spring back to the One, like letting go a bit of elastic, self dies, which to us is death in advance—till we do it, when it becomes Life known for the first time.

But what courage to let go! To leap over the precipice with no guarantee you will survive; to fall into the darkness without any assurance that underneath are in fact the Everlasting Arms. This for you is to burn your insurance policies, destroy your principles and almost your reason. Are you girded for this journey? With self and all your belongings ready to hand over where you get your ticket? Are you willing to pay in advance, in faith, and no more, that in exchange, at the end of a long, hard road, Mr Lumley Brampton, O.B.E. will—what? Get Zen? No, but perhaps in a moment of supreme unawareness hear laughter in strange places, good fat belly laughter, and see the smile of God in all about you, and be for the first time happy, and careless, and made free.

I apologise. I have bullied you, lectured at you, shouted at you. But I see you—if you will permit the rude disclosure—as a proud animal, mature yet powerful, prowling a self-made Zoo. *I* cannot let you out, but perhaps I can help you to realise that you are in a cage to which you have the only key.

In this belief I sign myself your friend,

Christmas Humphreys

Dear Martha,

I am glad your immediate troubles with the children are over. Now
you say that you have for the moment time for Zen. You are stepping
off on the wrong foot. Zen is not an additional activity, to be added
to a husband, two babies and a home. *Zen does not exist*, so put that
in your cigarette holder and smoke it instead of your usual twenty
a day. There is no such thing as the pursuit of Zen or studying Zen
or acquiring Zen. Zen *is*; all that changes with success is that one
day we shall *know* it. Now we only believe it and that not very
strongly. If you can't see Zen in washing up or potting the baby
you won't see Zen in Suzuki's eyes, as a new awakening. It produces
a new scale of values, of what is important and what is important
more, a new meaning for happiness. It is not a release from
suffering, large or small, but its utter acceptance, and in that
acceptance its defeat. We suffer still, but oh, how differently! Here
is a 'sitting loose to life' in Geraldine Coster's immortal phrase.
Thoughts arise; we greet them, use them and say goodbye. In the
same way loves and hates and fears arise. They are treated with care,
as an entomologist would examine a fly that alights on his desk.
But finding he did not want it he would let it fly away.

When the hands that hold are opened, and let go,
And thought, a blown leaf on the winds of circumstance,
Lies still, and dies untenanted,
So life that sweetly sang within its veins,
New given back to earth, shall there
Be fetterless, unriven, free . . .

(I apologise. My new silent typewriter, known of course as
William, gets like this in the spring!)

So start again. You don't 'give time' to Zen; you find that you
have time for nothing else. And if the name bothers you call it
something else. It is not new or Japanese or queer. If you like, call
it Fiddle-de-dee, and we will all be Fiddle-de-Deists. Look up
chapter XXV of your *Tao Tê Ching*.

There is a thing inherent and natural
Which existed before heaven and earth . . .

I do not know its name.
If I am forced to give it a name
I call it Tao . . .

But you needn't give it any name, just sing. Do face that fact that
Zen is, and a touch of it changes nothing yet makes all things new.
Then truly the morning stars sing together, and darning socks is
mending the normal wear and tear of the universe. You hate shelling
peas? I will give you an exercise. Start shelling peas. Now you are
God creating new thoughts for the salvation of mankind. Create
some and flick them into the bowl. Now drop the symbolism and
just shell peas. Now drop yourself in with the peas and—let me
know the result.

Yours in the joy of shelling,

T.

LETTER 3

Dear Zelnuk,

You clearly have a first-class brain and have read very widely of
Western thought. You quote conclusions and comparisons but
I must confess I cannot follow you, for I have never read one word
of it. For some reason the Heart Sutra, or the heights of Kegon
philosophy delight me; western philosophy is to me the piling of
dead flowers, or bricks of clay that have no light in them. Some
great conclusion is reached, and I yawn and say, 'So what?', whereas
one line of the *Tao Tê Ching* or the *Voice of the Silence* lights up
the darkest day. So pity me in my ignorance, but allow me to
dogmatise (what blasphemy!) from the point of view of Zen. You
say you will now tackle Zen, but you will clearly attempt to use the
same equipment as that which you successfuly used to scale the
heights of Kant and Hegel, whoever they were. It just won't do.
Do get clear (the concept) that Zen is beyond all concepts,
beyond all thought. No thinking achieves Zen, only more and more
about it. Books are all about it, certainly mine and even Dr Suzuki's,
to the extent that words are symbols of concepts and therefore of the
stuff of relativity. The bricks by which we build in thought are
thought-forms, things created by thought as bricks are made in
moulds by man-power used on the physical plane. These thought-
things, things made of thought, are made of the substance of thought,

53

which is substance or matter on the plane of thought as clay is matter on the physical plane. Rules are devised by men for the use of the thought-forms thus created. We build up symbols and analogy, language and elaborate reasoning. For straight-forward production of a conclusion we use logic, as a scientist uses a slide rule. For abstract thoughts we use metaphysics, though what man thinks he gains by chopping up thought in this way I know not. You might as well cut up the sea with a bread knife. Let psychology be the laws of the machine of the mind, and mysticism the technique of direct vision of Reality and its subsequent expression, and so on. But are you one inch nearer to Truth or only formulating ideas about it?

However, this is your field and not mine. All I say is that from the Zen point of view, as I understand it, these are so many boxes, variously coloured if you will, but prisons, tombs. Surely a conviction means that some noble idea has died, a conclusion is something shut up, and therefore dead, a dead-end. And even a principle which runs on tram-lines, like a cab-horse in blinkers, will never leave the earth and soar and sing in the golden light of the morning?

No, the only way out of thought is to think to the end of thought. Think to the precipice where logic dies, and the last thought has ending. Just believe, as a hypothesis, that there is something beyond sense, a divine non-sense where A is A, as Dr Suzuki points out, but equally A is not-A. Is this untrue? But surely if anything is true, so is its opposite, else the true were only half true? There cannot be good without evil, nor light without shadow, and we know heat but by its absence, cold. Surely the universe, whatever else it is, is harmony incarnate. It is *all*, and therefore the balance of all parts. But the parts are crystallised out, as it were, in pairs of opposites. Concepts are built up of opposites into convenient units of thought made up of the choice of so many of so many pairs. All thought is comparative. How, then, can we usefully say that Zen is anything, or try to catch it with the butterfly nets of the professor? Nor will it yield to the bird-lime of paradox, though some in this way have caught its tail. But seriously, supposing you say that Zen is 'absolute idealism mystically experienced,' what have you said, what have you got?

Think this over, but better still, try to intuit it, to see, with a yelp of delight, if you permit yourself such joy, that it is true. Then we can begin.

   Yours, not yet out of the net of thinking,

LETTER 4

Dear Rodney,

Do be your age. You write like a love-sick school-boy to a famous
film-star. I am not your Guru just because I take a class in the
approach to Zen, nor are you my *chela* in the profound spiritual
sense of that Indian term. The Indian relation between master and
pupil is often that described as Bhakti Yoga, the way of devotion
to a personified Ideal, often in the person of the Teacher. That is
not the Zen way, where the master is much more impersonal (more
like Jnana Yoga in Hindu terms), and more like the western
psychiatrist. True, the psychiatrist is only dealing with the
machinery of the mind, and matters of *satori* and the like are utterly
beyond his ken, but like the Zen master he holds up a mirror to the
pupil-patient's mind in which he can the more easily see his own
mind, and hence its limitations, aspirations and best method of
progress. The Zen master, and hence all below him in rank who
even breathe the word Zen to a class, is solely concerned to help
the student break through the limitations of thought to his own
enlightenment. He gives him nothing, passes nothing. Why? There
is nothing to give.

   So it is no good clamping onto me, or some marvellous new book
or person or idea. Stand on your own feet, for if you do you will
for the first time be happy, and incidentally a most rare person.
Most of us lean back, into the past, or forward, into an idealised
future, or cling to support on either side. Or we fear the future, and
so, in facing it lean back and move to it fearfully. Or we run from
the past, or from the present, endeavouring to escape to some other
place, or time, or circumstance. There are no other places, for we
are always here wherever we are, and it is always now, at all times.
So stand up and accept things as they are. Others will help you to
find the Truth within—you, but *you* must find it. Be a vast rock
in a stormy ocean, and let others seek refuge in you, or in your lee.
But that won't do either, for the rock is moving with the storm!
Rock, storm and sea, the seekers of refuge and the well-content,

we are all moving, changing, but moving nowhere, for there is nowhere to move . . . All right, get on with your work for you do it splendidly; and let us be colleagues and not a limpet and a rather weary rock in a very muddled sea!

Good typing,

LETTER 5

Dear Miss Melland,

You do not need to tell me that you are desperately in love. Ça se voit, as the French say. Of course love is wonderful. It makes the world go round, so they say, though the Theravadin Buddhists would shake their heads and say, 'That is the trouble.' It keeps the Wheel of Life revolving with the karmic consequences of this personal desire, ever renewed, never satisfied. But a fat lot that will worry you on your honeymoon! And don't let it, say I. Being in love may be a functional neurosis but nature invented it, and I see no point in calling her handiwork rude names. But when you recover from this endemic and ever-prevalent disease you will appreciate (as George, with a milder attack, does already), that this is a disease to be enjoyed and cured of—after which there will be time for Zen. I know that I have often said there is nothing outside the ambit of Zen, and it is to be found in licking stamps as in founding Empires, but at least the gents involved in these several enterprises are reasonably sane . . . I say no more. So get on with your mutual adoring, get married, and come gently back to earth, to the nobler relationship of mutually understanding, reasonably and periodically passionate, friends. But meanwhile don't drag Zen into it. The Zen master would I think send you away on the ground that you do not at present want Zen, you want a double bed. Well, get into it. In Buddhism there is no sin, only consequences, and I look forward to the appearance of the first of them. After that, thirty blows for the mind which strays from its theme or exercise!

Yours remembering,

LETTER 6

Dear Bungy,

Why is it I can't find Zen material in the Class, or is it I can't see it under my nose? Love-sick maidens, Guru-hunting youths,

56

retired business men who study Zen like a Company prospectus, and housewives who in a full day allocate time for Zen between bathing baby and welcoming hubby home . . . where is the English equivalent of the eager, merry, fierce-minded horde of young Japanese students that I lived with and meditated with in the Zen monasteries of Japan?

I look at thirty faces, so many masks for thirty minds—all unreal, like I that look at them, yet at the same time sparks of the Flame, facets of the one Life, and just so many 'continua of non-contiguous thought-moments in a force-form-time field of discrete phenomena,' or some such bleary verbiage. Life must have hiccups of laughter at times at the silly noises we make about her! We may be merely that, but I prefer us as Martha and Rodney and the unsmiling Mr Brampton and the ever-smiling Mrs Wilmer who has got it all. But how can I reach these minds with mine? When I look at them I see an elderly balding man, or a young and very pretty girl, or a plump and comfy blonde 'd'un certain age' with an intellect like a high-power sports car zooming round me in three dimensions. I must see deeper than this to the Self which is one with my Self, and in the light of the All-SELF equally non-existent. It gets easier with practice, for I suppose we must develop the muscles of the intuition as those of the biceps with deliberate use. All of us are seeking the Father, all are unhappy parts that yearn to go home. But how to start these dear folk on the way to Zen? Many are still miles from the entrance to that Way, many haven't the mind to think, much less to pass beyond the confines of that mighty faculty. May be I have found the entrance, but I claim no more. How, then, do I help them to it, and then push them through?

I suppose, first, by being utterly true to myself. As some wag said when I regretted I was not a better teacher, 'we have got the teacher we deserve, no better,' which was excellently and rudely true. If I give what I am I can give no more. 'Love thou me for what I am, so shalt thou find me fairest' is true, but if I tried to show off, be more than I am, teach what I know not, I should be false to the most sacred trust in the world, that between teacher and taught. I feel sometimes that I am the led not the leader, that I am panting along behind your remarkably swift advance to the experiences I talk of but have little known. All right, thank you for your advice. True, you have given none but you have helped by letting me let off this untidy steam.

Yours on the Path, and to hell with unbelievers,

LETTER 7

Dear Madam,

It is not easy to grasp your question. Perhaps it is not very clear to your own mind, and it has been said that only the perfectly formulated question can be answered, and that when it is perfectly put it needs no answer. (You are right, that is one of those profound sayings which may be true but is not very helpful.) I think what you are asking is why isn't goodness enough to secure enlightenment? This is a big question and might need a long answer. It is the why that may be difficult. The fact is surely plain. There are many, many good people about us, sound in ethics, conduct and character, who are yet nowhere at all on the way to enlightenment. These good people pursue the Good as others the Beautiful or the True, to use the old formulae, but Raj Yoga, the supreme Yoga with its Wisdom (*Jnana*), Devotion (*Bhakti*) and Action (*Karma*) Yoga has all three. The good alone will never include the true, for they are the reflections of different faculties, as it were. The saint need not be learned or even wise, the intellectual genius may not be at all good, but one touch of Zen experience is beyond good/evil, beyond true/false, out of time. Of course, this does not mean that it is waste of time to dominate the lusts and frailties of the flesh, to develop patience, compassion, humility. All this *must* be done, *sometime* by *all*. But if you seek Zen, and you may not be wise in doing so yet, you seek that desperate flash of the Absolute in which heaven and earth are both consumed and both are born anew. Thereafter you *know*, and as such are purged of the conceit of self and the danger of being content with the Good *or* the Beautiful *or* the True. You will want, and become all of them, and that which lies beyond—no less—and that is not describable.

You are a noted novelist. You therefore have a powerful imagination. Follow me. Think of *NOTHING*, and enter it. No sight, sound, thing about you. Space, darkness, eternity. It *is not*, nor can you know that you are you. In the absence of difference nought knows that it is;—there is no self-consciousness. Difficult to realise? It is impossible! Now Non-dual becomes—not Two yet—

but One. (You remember Eckhart's distinction of the Godhead beyond God?) For the One is conceivable and the Absolute is not. It is this One that becomes Two, Three and then 'the ten thousand things.' Now back again. From the many to the few, the few to Two, the Two to One, and then? Jump, JUMP! Well, it can't always come off but one day it will. And then? You won't need words from me. But meanwhile to move to the Good is enormous wisdom, for it ensures right motive for all our acts, and, more important, for all our desire. *Why* do we want anything, even Zen? Who can answer that faithfully and not be ashamed of the reply? For self, for Self, for all mankind, or for no reason at all, Zen's 'purposelessness?' If this is all too high for you drop it, and read it again in a year.

Till then,
Yours sincerely,

LETTER 8

Dear Mary,

You have so much to offer, you are so beautiful of form and mind, why spoil yourself for us with such sad blemishes? Jung would call you an introvert, and in his famous diagram would classify you as an intuitive emotional. As such you are rare in England, as a developed mind. At the same time you have a deep compassion for all forms of life, not as a mere intellectual idea but as a force of character. Why, then, and you ask me to be frank, spoil all this with so much spiteful criticism of others? Why write me four pages, two of deep stuff and two of catty, useless hurting attacks on other members of the group? It can't be jealousy, and you aren't the hating type. I must take you up on this because I have used the word hurting advisedly. Thoughts do injure, and can injure gravely. This applies anywhere, but in a small group, which should be as the fingers of one hand, the injury is greater, to the individual and to the group. I can't let it go on. Thoughts of illwill are like arrows, with venomed points. They stick in, and fester, and believe me, it is a strong mind that, receiving them perpetually, can remain unaffected.

Can't you accept in fact, as you must in principle, that others with different views, on doctrine, technique of meditation, or what-

59

ever it may be, are just as likely to be right as you—for them, now, here? You would claim that you allow them their point of view. But you won't *accept* it, in the sense of giving way to it, digesting it, absorbing it, and genuinely accepting that it *may* be true, or as partially true as your own opinion. But grudgingly to allow the other man to exist is not to allow him tolerance, save in the sense of impatiently putting up with. That is not tolerance. You have heard me quote, and I will quote again, a phrase I heard Annie Besant use, 'True tolerance is an eager and a glad acceptance of the way along which others seek the truth.' Think it over.

But perhaps I am being hard on your conscious mind. It may be that your venom, particularly against Sally, comes from the sub-conscious or unconscious part of the mind. Your remarks about her sound like a Victorian school-maam. Supposing she has 'boy-friends.' Surely that is her affair, not yours. I know about them and it does not worry me. Her sex-life is her own affair, and not (thank Karma) any of mine. Or yours. Or *are* you jealous? (I can see you getting scarlet at that one.) But what if she wrote to me of you, of your moods and sulkiness, and your spite at her? Can't you accept her with her failings as you presumably accept me with mine? Knowing too well my own moments of self-doubt and depression, of inconsistency of mood and purpose, now violent, now piano, now boisterous-whimsical and now sheer school-boy, I can easily accept others' weakness. Can't you? Do try. If we all took off not only our clothes but our bodies, and all the silly little habits of behaviour and attitude to people and circumstance, would you dislike us all so much? Or any of us? Or Sally?

Is this but a moral lecture? Not in the least. But you say you want Zen, and I am leader of a class of such. I say you will not find Zen while filled with a sense of separation, of barriers of criticism and dislike, intellectual, moral and almost physical, between yourself and other members of the Circle. Zen is beyond distinctions, large or small, beyond you and Sally, utterly beyond me.

The change for the better can I think be sudden. I hope I am not being blasphemous, but I think I see how miracles are sometimes wrought. I think you have reached the end of this particular weakness, and a mere shrug of the shoulders will shrug it off. Just suddenly take Life in your hands and hug it. Let it sing to you, play with you, play the fool with you. The sun is all about you, and beauty and light and fun. Drop the rest, the cloudiness, the grubbiness. Robe yourself in your own beauty of mind as well as body. So, it is done. It is well. Congratulations!

Yours brutally, with love,

LETTER 9

Dear Silver,

It was good of you to say so much. If at 22 you are on your way to a medical degree, and have found time to read so much of comparative religion and philosophy and in particular so much of Buddhism and Zen I congratulate you. At your age I had done the same, and at Cambridge too, but then I read Law and never did more than five hours work a day. You for Medicine have to work eight, or your father's generation did in my time. But now you want proof that satori, which you call the experience of Zen, is not merely subjective. Wow! This wants a lot of sorting out, but if you have time to put your question I suppose I must find time to answer it.

Let us begin at the end. Subjective, yes, if such a distinction is valid. It is certainly not objective in the usual sense of the term. 'Merely' subjective? I see the trap before me. At its face value your question may be answered, yes, as before. But perhaps you really want me to agree that it is a glorified hallucination, as a ghost is said to be merely subjective (though to me as objective as a cat, though of finer matter). But by western rules of thinking you are surely begging the question, for satori is *ex hypothesi*, i.e. by definition (as if that were possible with satori!), that which is of the Absolute, and therefore beyond the limitations of the relative. In other words, if it is hallucination it is not satori; if it is satori, if it *is*, it is not any sort of hallucination, 'mere' or otherwise. It is like the intuition, the faculty of satori. One test of intuitive knowledge is that it gives a sense of absolute certainty. If doubt remains it is not the intuition speaking, even though reason cannot yet express the certainty in terms of the intellect. But as such it is, and must be, incapable of proof. If a man draws a gun and fires point-blank at his enemy and the enemy falls dead with a bullet in the heart that is pretty good proof that he killed the man—at least good enough for most Old Bailey juries. But if I say that Life is one, or that Karma and Compassion are at cosmic level expressions of the same 'divine' or cosmic harmony, I *know* that to be true, but I can't prove it to you and I wouldn't try to do so.

So let's drop proof. As I have often said, nothing worth proving can be proved. Meanwhile the baby chuckles and grabs what it likes the look of, perhaps the cat's tail; the bird in the tree squawks to keep another cat away from its nest, and you sun yourself in the same sun in the same garden. Life goes on, using a million forms and wearing them all out, in a second as with a microbe or in a million years or so as with a mountain. You too are Life in a perishable set of forms, and when Life has used you she will put you in the dust-bin and walk on. And Zen? Is THAT made manifest, whence or how or why or when it matters not, nor would the Buddha discuss such matters as having no relation to the whole-time task of walking on and walking on, out of the house of self and into Enlightenment. Zen *is*, in all things and events and circumstances. Accept it so, with all your senses, but closing gently for a while the steel doors of your analytic, separative mind. For the moment accept Life—you may study her later. Fall in love with her, caress her and be caressed in turn, or be chastised by her, but don't only look at the woman with a desire to pull her to pieces. Come off the cold, proud pedestal of western thought. "Be humble," says the Tao Tê Ching, you will remember, "and you will remain entire." That is one of the greatest remarks ever made. Humbly unseparate, contentedly part of an endless and undifferentiated All, live life at times, *live* it, and in greater humility thereafter tear the woman to pieces if you must, to see what makes her tick.

No, there is no proof of Zen, or of Life itself for that matter. The only proof for you is your experience and for me mine. But when you have it, and another asks for proof, or even for a description of the experience, you will just smile, not a superior smile but the gentle grin as of friends who share a common secret, and one which has made and will forever make all things as new.

Your friend to be,

LETTER 10

Dear Martha,

I am glad to hear you are getting on so well 'inside' and 'outside', as you put it. So you are 'zenning' your cooking, your shopping and even the baby. Excellent. As Dr Suzuki wrote, 'There is nothing infinite apart from finite things.' If only one could see the infinite in the finite! I remember gazing a long time at an ash-tray, wondering what spring in my mind I could find and touch which would make the ash-tray reveal its primordial and unstained infinity. In the end I came to the conclusion it was the use of the word 'my' in connection with mind. I haven't got one, and to the extent that I have the ash-tray remains as such, and no more.

But now to your worries. Psychic visions. See what they are (and I don't mean their infinity). The engineer is told of a weird noise in the engine, and sets to work to find out what it is that causes it. First, you don't of course see them at all with the eye. You would see as much, as you almost admit, with your eyes shut. Nor are the visions mental, in the sense of created thought-forms. Still less are they hallucinations. No, you are entering at times willy-nilly a new world, as real as the physical or the mental but of the substance of neither. It is like finding an entresol between the ground and first floors. This psychic plane is neither good nor bad, but because we are for the most part grossly ignorant of it, it is apt to be dangerous. Forms are enormously different and in one sense reversed, as though seen in a mirror. Colours are far more real, being 'seen' as of living substance and not the reflection of light. The human faculty for contacting this plane is a body made of its substance, as our physical body is used to contact the physical plane. Its substance is seen as starry, hence, presumably, the word astral adopted at one time in the Theosophical movement. This astral double of the physical is the true seat of the physical senses, and of the 'lower *iddhis*' or abnormal (but never supernatural) powers of clairvoyance, clairaudience, psychometry, etc. Heavy-handed scientists are now solemnly proving that people can communicate 'mentally' at a distance, which every savage tribe has known since the world began, and also thousands in the West, not to mention the millions of the East, until the scorn of their elders (but not betters) knocks the knowledge out of them. E.S.P. (Extra-sensory-perception) is a high-faluting name for the deliberate transmission of knowledge from a positive to a negative mind, which several of us at Cambridge forty years ago would practise as an amusing exercise round the fire. One person would strongly visualise, say, the steps of St Paul's Cathedral, and the others, making their minds blank screens, nearly always picked it up, or very near it. And so on. But I have no time to talk at length on a matter so unimportant, and having no bearing whatsoever on Zen attainment. But read it up in Dr L. J. Bendit's *The Psychic Sense*, or *This World and That*, both published by Faber. I knew him well at Cambridge, and later his wife Phoebe Payne with whom he collaborated. This will tell you more of 'psychic powers' so-called, and the danger of them. But the danger of their abuse is well rubbed in in *The Voice of the Silence*. Much of the Deva or 'angel' evolution, parallel to humanity, functions on this plane, and fairies of all kinds belong to it. But most small children at one time or another pass through a phase of having the 'sight,' and can see these things and people. Then they grow out of it or, as I have said, get smacked out of it, and forget. Or do they? I didn't. And the Celtic races, Irish, Highland Scots, Bretons and so on, are naturally psychic at all ages. So don't worry about your 'sight.' Ignore your visions of colour-forms and the like, and go on to develop, at their level of existence, far higher faculties. Including the intuition, which must never be confused with psychic 'feeling,' the seat of many of our 'hunches', as of many of our sudden likes and dislikes of people and places. Of the foul practice of spiritualism, and the untold because unseen damage it does to the medium used, I may find time to speak later. Meanwhile walk on, and good shopping on the way.

LETTER II

Dear Mary,

Thank you for taking my rude letter so well. Now we can forget it. But I heartily agree that it is the silly small things about us that annoy each other so much. You can forgive a man for an arrogant manner if he has a great brain, or a woman's gush if she is really intuitive and has great things at times to say, but we squirm at the way a man sniffs before each utterance, or calls everyone dear old boy, or the woman who will not bath sufficiently or wears appalling hats. But I have a sneaking feeling that we also love one another for trivial habits which we find endearing, the little tricks of personality for which we want to hug each other because they make us feel happy. Or are these little tricks the windows through which we see in them the one Self which is in all of us, and a feeble reflection of the SELF or Absolute—(I shall call it the WHOO-HOO soon, as I'm tired of the other silly names)? I don't know.

But now for your 'new loneliness'. It isn't new but cyclic, and you had forgotten the earlier bout of it, as we forget the last go of 'flu. And you aren't any more lonely than before. We are always lonely in the sense that we are always, even to the end, alone. But the hell of loneliness is the feeling of separation, and this is illusion. Shall we say that we are holding hands in the darkness but at times it is so dark we cannot see the hands? But you can feel for them, and forgetting your want of a hand, offer one. We *are* our brother's keeper, and he needs us. Deplore the sin in him if you will, but never dislike the sinner. It is his giving way to the sin *that he may despise as much as you* that is his fault. The sin, being a temporary product of *avidya*, is common to us all. So are the virtues, but to borrow another's virtue, even though we basically have it too, is apt to make us conceited, so stick to the sins, even at the price of depression. For we are animals, and most of our sins are animal sins. But what is right for them is now wrong for us. The animals fight for food, or a cave to sleep in, or a mate, or to survive. So do we, but the fighting in us is not so pretty. The animal in us should now be at heel. An able, cultured middle-aged man is not a pretty sight when fighting, and dirtily fighting, another man, a dear friend, perhaps, for his wife or stamping out a poor little rival firm that only wanted to live, but was in the way of the larger one's ambitions. And women? Don't incite me to be rude. (Even) they will gain enlightenment, so they say, when they earn the right to male bodies . . .

But to be serious. Zen *is*, and we are in the way of ourselves. How to get out of our own way? One way is to be humble, a lot more humble, at least in our plans for our own attainment. Impatience is to my mind often a virtue, but I cannot join the many who, struck with the wish to achieve the summit of Everest, are pained to find they have not arrived a week or two later. Where is imagination, modesty, common sense? Before leaving the foothills there would be a thousand things to do, of training, route-planning, supplies. Most of us are bowled over by the first East wind on the first climb up some narrow, rocky, dangerous footpath at a mere 10,000 ft. And how many of us has ever stood at even 10,000 ft.?

E   65

(I scrambled up the hill-side, puffing and panting, in the Haute Savoie to feel I'd done it. Then I realised the fun was saying 'ten thousand', but to my French friends this is merely three thousand metres! So I came down again, to find my car was blocking a bus . . Oh, the ego!)

But we do have peeps of the high peaks now and again. We may sit in front of them, or even live in front of them yet see them seldom. Then suddenly a veil is drawn, without purpose, silently. The cloud is still solid, below, but there, so high it is almost over us, as we crane our necks and gasp, it is there—unbelievable, unutterable but there. And we stand and cry, and care not that we cry, and we do not forget.

Meanwhile know that you *can* do whatever comes to be done. What comes to be done is duty; it would not be there to be done unless you had made it so. So do it. You may fail, but failure is nothing. But to stop trying would be awful, as W. Q. Judge wrote in his *Letters that have helped me*. And he goes on, 'We have not a clear road. No, it is not clear. I am content if I can see the next step in advance only.' So am I, for it is generally as much as I can tread.

Sorry for such a long letter, but as I see more clearly myself I find that it helps to write it down. You are the victim this time. But much loved by your tormentor,

LETTER 12

Dear Zelnuk,

I admire the courage of your efforts to get out of your bonds of thought. Houdini never got out of worse than you have coiled about your free, intuitive mind. But if you use your mind you will see that you are still creating as many bodies as you dissolve. For Zen is the direct path; it ignores all mediates, all veils of concept or emotion or valuation. Consider the fencer. He sees his opportunity. Ping! A hit! Did he consider what to do, choose a method of attack, work out the movements necessary and then lunge? He did not. He hit. True, the hitting was the result of a very compound cause of a trained eye and wrist and much knowledge. Having achieved all this he forgot it—and hit. You are still perpetually striking intellectual attitudes. If I say to you relax, you promptly produce a syndrome of thought *about* relaxation, its advisability, technique, advantages. But I did not say, think about relaxing. I said relax. Now go for a walk. I said, GO! I didn't say work out the most advantageous method of putting your hat on! And so on.

You scientists (and for that matter Theravada Abhidhamma technicians) take a flower and tear it into its components. Where is the flower? Ha, they say, triumphantly, that is just what we were pointing out. There isn't one. Bosh, say I, picking up another and enjoying its beauty, its fragrance, its floweriness, content with what it *is*. But what is enjoying it, they ask? I am, say I, and to hell with niceties of concept, not all of which shall rob me of the moment of awareness, the moment of unutterable life when the flower and I lie undivided on the altar of the Ever-living. Sorry, I get poetic at times when I get my mouth full of the dust of concept. For it is so sterile, so unutterably dead. I feel like a laughing harlot on the doorstep of a pure Professor of the Good . . . So, the mood passes, and to pay my grocer's bill I must descend again to concept. But will you not come alive at times, feel happy, silly, childish once again—and even laugh—fat, belly-laughter as of a man made free? Then we will sing together, and get drunk together and together pluck the fruits of folly in the garden of the Real.

Yours more deeply than may seem,

LETTER 13

Dear Mr Gunther,

You must really allow me, in reply to your letter of the 13th February, to answer in the Zen manner. Zen experience is utterly, totally and for all time beyond the utmost reach of thought, and therefore, of concept. I cannot, therefore, as a student of Zen, waste time considering such vague abstractions as "lucidity without ideation". The Zen Masters, hearing such a phrase, would hit the speaker on the head. Nor is it possible to consider what remains unattached and what is the awareness of being unattached in avoiding attachment to thought. Surely you can see that so long as there is thought, there is attachment, and anything which is aware of not being attached to something else is still in the realm of duality. Zen is not concerned with the realm of duality. It is concerned with the realm of non-duality, and all this playing about with concepts may be talking about Zen but it is not Zen and will not lead to it.

To regard Zen Buddhism as a new system of thought is to miss the point of its existence. It exists to the extent that it helps the genuine student to break through the barriers of thought and achieve a blinding flash of im-mediate, instantaneous awareness of non-duality. All else is chatter and a waste of time.

Yours sincerely,

LETTER 14

Dear Mr Tolson,

Please don't sneer at yourself as a teacher, as 'a mere don'. There is no greater occupation for a human being than to teach. The teacher-healer-priest should be one, and once they were, in Babylon. All alike from greater knowledge (Knowledge) help the pupil-patient-penitent to know more of himself and thereby to achieve his own health-integration-salvation. The priest spoke for God, the doctor (psychiatrist) for the Whole-Health, the One-Mind, and the teacher for the inner Laws which create and control all outer facts. As such they were collectively the voice of Karma-Compassion-Harmony, for these three, as you will find if your meditation is deep enough, are one. And this triple man, a mighty man, was, is and always will be judged by what he is as much as by what he teaches. His example in the long run is the force by which he heals.

What higher role has man? To govern has always been regarded as inferior. In India the Brahmin is higher than the Kshatriya, the fighter-ruler. The Archbishop is always the power behind the throne. You teach what you know, which is partly what you were taught and partly what you rediscovered for yourself. Thus knowledge circulates, for blood must flow. At Cambridge, as wherever there is teaching, the many look up to the few, the taught to the teachers. But the few are dedicated to the many, and all who graduate feel the sacred tie to those who come after, to go back to teach, if requested, what they learnt. The room in which the teacher meets the taught is in fact a temple, for in it is the direct transmission of the knowledge (at low levels), Wisdom (at high levels) handed down, a sacred heritage, and the principle is the same as that of the Guru of India who, seated in the shade of a tree, teaches his pupils

68

patiently, unceasingly, the wisdom for which they are ready, no less and no more. What is taught is the same Truth, of the relation of Spirit to forms, and in the course of it *Buddhi* is developed to arouse the *Bodhi* asleep within. Did the Buddha do more? Only in quality, quantity and degree. So please don't be so rude to yourself. We must all teach what we know, else we do not deserve to learn more. As we empty ourselves of self we become a larger conduit pipe for the Wisdom, and so teach more. But we shall not enlarge that pipe by failing to appreciate the splendour of its function. Teach on; we can none of us do more; we should none of us dare to do less than try.

Your fellow teacher,

LETTER 15

Dear Rodney,

How can you help your friend who is going blind? In lots of ways. But first, do shut up gazing at me and writing to me as if I were the Guru of Gurus. I am not Christ nor do I work miracles. My purpose is single, to try to help fellow sufferers help themselves out of suffering. I stuff back the yearning for help into their own minds, so that they can see there is no help to be obtained, save from inside. 'Look within, thou *art* Buddha'—you have heard me quote that from *The Voice of the Silence* a dozen times. 'Come unto me', said Jesus, but the 'me' is not Jesus, it is the Christ-Principle, which is the Buddha-Principle within each one of us. 'I and my Father are one' is the Christ speaking, the faculty of Enlightenment which learns to know that it is enlightened already.

And so to your friend. The causes are of course physical and karmic, part on the physical plane, part on the inner planes working out onto the outer plane, like worry ending by making you sick. The effect must be endured and if possible used to planned purposes. When I was at Cambridge I rowed so hard I busted my back. Excellent, as I realised later. No more fierce exercise so I had time to read and meditate. And so to Buddhism and the Buddhist Society . . . Your friend must be, like the song of the Blind Ploughman which I sang when young in my deep bass rumble, 'God has taken away my eyes that my soul might see.' (Though I could never reach the high note of 'soul', which is perhaps symbolic).

69

So now you must prepare the old lady. Help her to face the situation and accept it, as distinct from being dragged, as it were, unwillingly to blindness. If she can cease to fear it she can the more easily prepare for it, as no more than losing a front tooth or the front bedroom to a lodger. All very easy for me to talk, you say? It is, for I have done it, that is, been nearer to blindness than she has. I've been blind, deaf, crippled, disgraced, in prison, and been given six months to live. You will have read that the Japanese samurai as part of their training would 'die' before they ever went into battle. By strenuous meditation, use of the imagination and so on, they learnt to have 'died', to have flung away the body in the service of their Lord, before a blow was struck. As such they were all but invincible, for they had nothing to lose. So I at least in imagination, and scores of times have planned my life anew on the basis that I had just had the news. 'You're blind, you're disgraced, you're going to prison for five years.' I've even worked out a meditation system for my cell, and was able to hand it over at once to a member of the Society who is in fact doing five years for burglary. He reports great success, and has interested the Chaplain and two Prison Visitors . . . After such preparation I found that when given a month's notice from a job I'd held for twenty-five years—and thought I held for life—I felt no shock whatsoever beyond a mild reaction of 'What damned impertinence!' I worked out a new career within twenty-four hours and was soon impatient to begin.

So get the old lady to accept herself as blind already, to plan for Braille, touch-typing, reading by being read to and using the radio intelligently as never before. Treat the loss of sight as the loss of a leg, and not as semi-death. Attack the crisis positively instead of moaning negatively. Thus she can achieve a dynamic acceptance, which is rare and so much better than lying down flabbily to the will of an extra-Cosmic God who seems in need of psychiatry. And what a chance for Zen! I almost envy her, for it is so much easier to see Zen in a new situation than in the dreary round of the old!

Yours from the darkness,

70

LETTER 16

Dear Brampton,

You ask me yet again, What is Zen? What do you want me to say?
I know you have read half a dozen books on Zen Buddhism, and
even attended a meeting or two of the Class. Yet still you ask the
question which cannot be answered. What is it you want? A word,
a name, a sacred formula? Or a definition? But to define is to limit
(indeed *finis* is an end), and that which is limited is not Zen. What
would you say if *I* asked *you*, What is life? I know no useful answer.
It is a force, yes, utterly impersonal, cosmic in scope, which uses
all forms, large and small, and discards them when worn out. It is
the growth in crocuses and in the snow-flake, also that in the cancer
cell. It motivates sweet youth in love, and also venereal disease.
It produces the Aurora Borealis and the thought which created
Belsen. Vast or minute in the form it uses, creating (and destroying
with its remorseless pressure) the microbe and the mountain range,
intolerably patient as the mistress of all time, it moves the tides
and the sun and the earth; it makes the grass grow and my beard.
It breaks the brick wall with soft roots of creeper and hides the ruin
with unnumbered flowers. It shows in all of us as love and hate and
laughter; it is most alive of all in the festering corpse. But WHAT
IS IT? Tell me that and I will tell you what is Zen.

Yours peevishly perhaps, but very reasonably,

LETTER 17

Dear Silver,

I am glad you see what I mean when I say that Zen can never be
'proved'. And I admire your frankness in saying that to approach
it you can only use the car you have and not borrow someone else's.
All right, let us start again from there. Let us look at this car.

First, you have inherited it in the sense that you have not wrought
it in this present birth. Your present capacities, limitations, pre-
dilections, qualities and powers of thought and feeling, 'good' or
'bad', make up the car or 'vehicle' (the analogy is excellent, for
yana means vehicle and the *Mahayana* you favour is the Great
Vehicle). Why have you got this car and not some other? Buddhists
would say that this compound of qualities is the child of a million

causes in past lives; in terms of mechanics, the resultant effect of manifold causes. But we inherited them from our parents, in the sense that a weak chest comes from mother and a love of medicine from father only in this sense, that we were drawn to that family for rebirth by lines of attraction of like to like. I, for example, am born into a long line of lawyers because I am of that type of mind and can learn more in it; I am not a lawyer because I am born into a line of lawyers. However, accept or reject that as you will, I want to make this point, that your vehicle is set in its capacities, etc., and that your life will tend to be that of the tram, on set lines, rather than the sporting car free of the roads to be terrifying as you are on Saturday afternoons. You have been nurtured in an atmosphere of orthodox medicine. Your reactions to all thoughts are therefore severely conditioned by that upbringing. You would find it difficult to look dispassionately at, say, herbalism, or osteopathy, because you have been subtly conditioned to sneer at anything so unorthodox. My point, as you will see, is that though you are young you are not nearly as able to change your lines of thought and reaction, your channels of knowledge, as you imagine. And if you are bound at your age, how much more are those who approach Zen in middle-age? If you are serious in your urge to Zen you must therefore acquire the habit of a direct approach, deliberately dropping the innumerable assumptions which make up the platform on the hillside from which you look out on the land below you, the hills about you and the heights as yet unclimbed above your head. You have a host of assumptions about the body, the emotions and the mind. Is the intuition even on your curriculum? I hope so, for it is the sole faculty, unless the wisdom of the East from time immemorial is at fault, by which you will ever KNOW Zen as distinct from knowing about it.

Face, then, that you have to cut new channels in the mind, as an engineer, who is controlling the fall of water when making new channels for a stream, must dig and cut and blast to prepare the way for the new line of force. This takes time, and patience, and may run counter to your present training. But it has to be done, for Zen, as you will by now appreciate, is a movement beyond limitations. Of course this is impossible, all consciousness must move according to some control, and the Zen ideal—'Let the mind alight nowhere'—is tremendously high and difficult. But every concept, including all beliefs, principles, conclusions and even working hypotheses, is a barrier, however light, in the way of Zen experience. But here's the point; only to the extent that one is bound to these concepts is one fettered by them. The Zen master himself may have his 'views', even political if he cares to waste the time, and I have no doubt, say, that Dr Hisamatsu, whom I think you heard at the Society last Easter would, as a world-ranking expert on Zen pictures, argue firmly with rival pundits on the comparative merits of various schools. But his life-force, so to speak, would not be tied up in the concepts; he would *use* such thoughts and still be free.

This is the difficulty with a mind that is powerfully intellectual, so to develop the intuition that it can use the vehicle of thought and yet be untrammelled by its limitations. Some minds are deep-set in their tramlines and cannot fly above them and be free. For Zen is poised above the opposites, as the gull, with effortless ease, rides the wind and uses it, and being unfettered when it alights, in that sense 'alights nowhere'. All very difficult but great fun. That is why the master will say to the pupil, quite 'right' in his conclusions but of course one-sidedly so, that he is wrong. 'How dare you say that snow is white?' he will roar at the terrified pupil. And how right he is, for it could not be white if it wasn't also black, as I think by now you see. I know that it follows that all that we say, or your lecturers say, is never more than half true, but that itself is true! But enough or I shall give you indigestion.

Yours freely,

LETTER 18

Dear Brampton,

You ask the relationship of God and Zen. Not easy to answer, for though Zen, being a new concept for the West, can be given a fairly clear meaning, God has as many meanings as there are Western minds. At the highest, as the 'Godhead' of Eckhart, it is the Absolute; at its lowest it is the venerable but highly peevish old gentleman with a long white beard as known to many in my youth. I don't know what the present children have in their mind for God—perhaps nothing. But to all of us God is a religious term, and implies, does it not, some Power which is powerful enough to have created the Universe, and yet in some way be personal enough

73

to reflect our human weaknesses and be on intimate terms with the individual's needs. This is rationally impossible but religiously perfectly possible. This Other Power is the Amida of Shin Buddhism, as distinct from the Self-Power by which the Rinzai Zen practitioner seeks and finds enlightenment. So far, then, Zen practice has no use for God, and I am choosing my words carefully. Zen finds no use for that concept. If it were useful it might be used, as any other device or means to an end, a raft on which to cross a river, then to be cast aside. Zen lays tremendous emphasis on the search within. Everything is within says the man of Zen, strength and weakness, good and evil, Reality and the way to it. The outside is only a projection of the inside, events are reflections of thoughts, things are thought-begotten. What this is in terms of Western philosophy I know not—perhaps Very Absolute Idealism! I know not, but in practical terms its meaning is clear. Look to nothing, no thing at all, and to no person or Person or God for help, light or salvation. Not even to a Zen Master for he can give you nothing, nothing save guidance, a suggestion of a foot put wrong, a hint as to a better way. With no prayer needed there is no need for One to whom to pray. Nor can I agree that the One Mind is God, as you imply. This syndrome of ideas and doctrines, Tathata, 'suchness', Sunyata, the 'void' and the One-Mind or Mind-only, or the Essence of Mind, these are terms which are certainly not religious and are not the equivalent of the Christian God. So in Zen you must travel alone, or whimsically admit that you cannot, like an early member of the Society in Paris thirty years ago, who told my wife and me confidentially that he was a good Buddhist, but he loved the Virgin and for the time being liked to keep her statue enshrined amid flowers in his room! He felt better when we confessed in turn that we always burnt a stick of incense before the shrine of St Christopher, the patron of travellers, on our safe arrival in France! So come to terms with your God concept. Is he now necessary to you, and if so as representing what? Aren't you strong enough now to stand alone? Try. The attempt will bring you fresh experience.

Yours Godfully,

LETTER 19

Dear Silver,

I think you appreciate well enough now that Zen cannot be compared to anything at all, and that you take it for what it is. But as you ask me to bear with you while you compare it with everything you know I will do so, though I may be brief and brutal in my comparisons. But now you ask, Are the Mahatmas of India, and in particular the two responsible for *The Mahatma Letters to A. P. Sinnett*, Zen Masters? This involves definitions, which I loathe, for there is no truth in them, but I will do my best.

I take a Zen master to be a man trained in the traditions and technique of the Zen School of Buddhism who has achieved his Enlightenment, has proved as much to *his* master, and gone through the further training which entitles him to teach. He is then a *roshi*, who may or may not be an Abbot, or hold any other office in a temple, and may not be a monk, or member of the 'Church' at all. Such is Dr Hisamatsu, who visited the Society at Easter, 1958. A Mahatma means *maha*, great, *Atman*, which is the Spirit in man of St Paul, the SELF incarnate in my terminology, or briefly, a great soul. The Indians call them Rishis but the Buddhist terms are far more vague. I think such a man is higher than the Arhat level of the Theravada School, for if we are going to be technical the Arhat is the fourth, and the Rishi or *asekha*, 'masterless', level one degree or stage or initiation higher. Bodhisattva is a far more casual term. It may mean the Buddha-to-be, and therefore, at least Arhat level, but it may be a term of high respect for one who is openly self-dedicated to working for humanity regardless of the needs of self. Such men are apt to be called Bodhisattvas, even as Gandhi was called Mahatma, as a popular tribute to his holiness of life and loftiness of aspiration.

The two Mahatmas of the Mahatma Letters were the Master Morya, a Rajput, and the Master Koot Hoomi, a Kashmiri Brahmin. Towards the end of last century they attempted to make known to the West an outline, however tenuous, of the esoteric (because at that time unpublished) teaching, as compiled and collated and checked by generations of such self-perfected men, on cosmogenesis and anthropogenesis. H. P. Blavatsky, a pupil of the Master Morya, who had trained her in Tibet, wrote this outline in her various

75

works of which the greatest was the *Secret Doctrine*, published in 1888 in two volumes. Meanwhile the two Masters made the remarkable experiment of corresponding with a gifted Englishman, A. P. Sinnett, then Editor of an Indian newspaper, and giving him by correspondence an outline of the doctrine which he collated and reproduced in a beautifully lucid book called *Esoteric Buddhism*. On Sinnett's death these Letters were published in volume form (as one of the Trustees for the book I am now editing a third edition) as *The Mahatma Letters to A. P. Sinnett*. These three books, therefore, all stem from the knowledge of those two Masters. But note that they were concerned with giving the West a new presentation of the immemorial wisdom, with doctrine rather than the way by which the individual might attain the level of their masterhood. With the way they were only primarily concerned in explaining to Westerners ignorant of its first principles the method of teaching used in the East from time immemorial, of the Guru-chela relationship and all that it implies. They were teaching would-be pupils what pupilage entailed, no more, and you will not find in these books a hand-book to the mind's development in Zen or in any other school of spiritual awareness. When I gave a talk in Karachi a long time ago on Buddhism and Theosophy I complained that Theosophy, the old name re-used for the ancient Wisdom, contained no specific way of life. 'It does not claim to,' gently said an old and extremely learned Theosophist. 'The religions and schools do that; Theosophy *is* the Wisdom.' So you will not find in the Letters any specific course of spiritual training, though I for one have found more help in them than in any book in the world save one, and that was a later work of 'H.P.B.', *The Voice of the Silence*, which she translated from an extremely ancient Buddhist Scripture well known in the esoteric schools of Tibetan Buddhism. Some are not impressed by it; my own copy, signed by the Dalai Lama, is all I take with me to read when I go long journeys. But that is by the way.

But the Mahatmas, or Masters of the Wisdom, or Brothers, (they have endless names in many languages), have at some time had their Enlightenment, and when they are teaching their pupils no doubt speak from the plane of Prajna as does a *roshi*, and what they teach will be the same. But to the extent that a *roshi* is contained in my definition, and belongs to a specific school and technique of self-achievement they are not *roshi*. Will that do? But read the section of the Mahatma Letters on Probation and Chelaship for yourself. Much of it is dead history, but the men mentioned, their successes and failures, are you and me, for there is but one human character, and when tested the true man appears. Ignore the word Theosophy, which in the last half century has acquired unfortunate accretions of meaning. The Letters are beyond the accidents of any 'movement', and talk of eternal things. Would that I knew a tithe of the Wisdom which the Masters gave to Sinnett, for in all Buddhism, as published, I find but a part of the titanic sweep of cosmic Wisdom which the Masters teach and practise in their ceaseless and deathless work for the spiritual salvation of mankind.

So that's that. Now get on with Zen, directly, fiercely and without comparison.

Yours Comparatively,

LETTER 20

Dear Brampton,

You find it strange that anything 'so dynamic and complete as Zen' should get on happily without a First Cause or a specified end. What I had to say to you about God was on the religious side; this is in the field of philosophy and therefore of the concepts of the intellect. But surely you now appreciate that First Beginnings and Ultimate Ends are both beyond the range of the intellect? We can know about it and about but we cannot *know* what preceded the first blush of the first dawn of manifestation. We can give it a name, but does that help? The Buddha said that speculation on these imponderables was waste of time, for the answer whatever it was helped not at all in the whole-time and immediate task of self-enlightenment.

Your query, 'what is satori?', though of course unanswerable is much more pertinent, for it may well be said that we ought to have some idea of the thing we seek. Well, looked at from the plane of duality, on which we now live, satori is a sudden break-through of consciousness from the world of dualism to absolute awareness of things as they are, beyond any distinction and the least trace of duality. Looked at from its own plane (and I can't),

77

it is presumably timeless, in that it takes place out of time, and its duration can therefore not be measured, and as it involves a complete merger of the knower and the known it follows that we shall not know when we are in it! But this at least gives us a criterion by which to measure the genuineness of any experience, for where the person concerned is consciously enjoying the experience it is not satori!

The difference between satori and Nirvana or Heaven or anything of that ilk is, as I understand it, this; first, that the former is only a foretaste, the beginning of true enlightenment and not the end. Secondly, it is attainable at any state of grace or morality or intellectual attainment, here in this world, and as easily when peeling potatoes as when meditating in a cloud of incense. Third, being a break-through to the Absolute, and nothing less, it is utterly beyond all trance-condition or other exalted state of the relative consciousness. That is why, to be technical, Dr. Suzuki insists that Prajna is far beyond that Dhyana or meditation which produces the quietness of Samadhi. Satori is known by all as a flash, timeless, complete, bearing its own authority, and stamped with such certainty as to place the knowledge so obtained beyond the reach of argument and discussion of any kind . . . The knower and the known are fused in one awareness. In that 'moment' self is not, nor knowledge. Satori *is* . . . But how useless are words. Walk on, and may you learn what I am talking about. After that we can but smile at one another, but as those who share a secret knowledge which is the light of life and maketh all things new.

Yours hopefully,

LETTER 21

Dear Martha,

You still seem a bit muddled as to what you want. I think you now appreciate that Zen is a whole-time job, and that is why the Zen masters insist on having their pupils' undivided attention for twenty four hours a day. You see that Zen is not a new activity to be fitted in with a dozen others, and not to be examined to see 'if there is something in it'. But do you yet know what you are trying to get? You know that it is within, and that it is your mind which must be adjusted to become consciously aware at will of its essential

78

nature. The difference between an enlightened and an unenlightened man is, as Hui Neng points out, that one knows that he is enlightened and the other does not.

But still you talk of study as though that in itself will lead you to Zen. It can't, can it? Study has its uses, first to assimilate the principles of the traditional Buddhist ways of thought; secondly, to use those principles to modify and perhaps replace the existing trends of thought, for they are often opposed to and incompatible with your upbringing. And thirdly, to develop the intuition by which alone you will in the end achieve satori. That is all. No knowledge of doctrine, however profound, will itself produce satori. For remember always that it is not a state of relative knowledge, however high, nor of understanding, however deep. In satori the self that studies ceases to be—you are merged with your subject of thought. Two has become one and therefore indescribable. Let me rub this in.

You know of what is called mystical experience, and Mary knows more of it first-hand. Mystics break through to a fused awareness of Self and Reality, finding the Ideal, often personified, within. Whether in a 'vision' or moment of ecstasy it is a moment which is timeless, of absolute awareness, and is akin, of course, to satori. This is why Zen Buddhism is sometimes called a school of Buddhist mysticism. This is utterly different from the 'knowledge' of the greatest scientist or thinker in the realm of concept, though the intuition illumines all great thought. These intellects know *about*—the mystic *knows*, and the Zen wallah in satori knows so fiercely that he does not know he knows! Why not? Because the knower is no more—he is merged with the knowledge. Thus you are trying to break through from the relative to the Absolute, from the everyday world based on comparisons to the inner world of the essence of things, from becoming to Being, from the forms of life, any of them, to the direct living of life itself. How? One practice is to regard the pairs of opposites perpetually as such, and the apparent distinctions between them as unreal. Take men and women. They are complementary, and neither is better, any more than night is better than day or positive better than negative in electricity. Effort and rest, strength and weakness, Jung's introversion and extraversion, these are pairs, like the two sides of a penny. If these do not quarrel as to which is the better, heads or tails, need we, with our intellect versus emotion, etc., quarrel? For these are one thing seen as two things in a world of relativity. We can see both of them one after another but never both at once (like the two sides of the coin). And the duality is all illusion. I like to visualise the universe as stretched between two poles—then I let go of the elastic suddenly. Ping! There's only ONE left. And where does the ONE go? Well, that's a Zen koan, as you know. Answer it and you have the secret of Zen.

Good hunting!

LETTER 22

Dear Silver,

I am glad you are 'wriggling out of the tramlines of thought'. (I wish I could do a drawing of you doing it). Now you most reasonably ask, why, if the object of the exercise, as you put it, is to free oneself from all fetters do I insist on members of my Class assuming a new set under the name of discipline? I will tell you. There are four main reasons. First, as a perpetual aid to working up and maintaining the state of being 'mindful and self-possessed' at all times of the day. If at some time into the day one packs one's breathing exercises (anyhow good for the health of all foul-air-breathing Londoners), a period of study, a period of meditation, the consideration of the fortnight's 'theme' at odd moments and the recollection of the Shrine at 12, 6 and 9, it helps one, so we find, to remain at least *less* attached to mundane affairs, and to shift the emphasis from money-grubbing or household chores to the movement of the higher mind towards enlightenment. Secondly, it is helping one to cut new grooves of thought towards a non-materialistic way of living, and to absorb and so apply these new ideas and values. Thirdly, it gives a needful stimulus to the habit of self-control which, useful and even necessary at all times, is even more necessary in Zen, and for this reason. At an early stage in Zen training one is apt to arrive at the dangerous half-truth, 'if all is unreal, all things illusion, good and evil just a pair of opposites and both no more important than the other, then what the hell?' What does it matter how we behave and what we do? This danger has long been foreseen and in the Zen temples guarded against. Dr Suzuki often refers to it as the danger of antinomianism. I looked this up and found the Antinomians were a sixteenth century German

sect who held that the moral law is not binding on Christians. So
there is the Awful Warning, and a little discipline prevents one
lapsing into that error. Finally, I think the practice helps one to
live the monastic or monkish life all day, not as kill-joy or dreariness
but, as W. Q. Judge put it, 'wearing the Yellow Robe internally.'

It may be true, as a most learned gentleman put it to me once
in class, that we only need to use this force to restrain ourselves
in adult life because of the wrong way we were handled in our
infantile desires when young. This may be so, but Zen starts
from where we are and not from where we ought to be. Like the
Buddhism from which it sprang it is scientific in this, that it begins
with facts as found, and develops thought and action from that
starting point. I can put it another way. We are all part animals.
I amuse myself at times looking at those about me as animals
rather cleverly balancing on two legs, and with their now hairless
bodies all dressed up like performing poodles, but still animals,
with animal necessities which are natural, and, what is more important, animal desires which are equally in one sense 'natural'.
Is this animal to be like an untrained randy fox-terrier, which chases
enemies, cats and girl friends as it pleases, and will not come to heel
when called, or is it to be as the centaur, one part of a twin-unit
of Mind-animal, as the union of spirit-matter, life and form,
the One manifest in the Many? If the latter is the higher ideal,
self-discipline intelligently self-applied must help towards it.
But it must be self-applied, for a known purpose and to a known end.
When no longer needed it is relaxed utterly. When the terrier will
come to heel when called he can be let off the lead.

Meanwhile start whistling and see what happens. The deafness
of *my* animal is quite amazing. As for the lead, one end is attached
to me—and the other? You wait till I *do* grab that animal . . .

Yours in need of discipline,

LETTER 23

Dear Mary,

Still that loneliness? You trouble me, for you know as well as I
that Life is one, and that all of us are truly 'members one of another'.
And you with your naturally mystical temperament know it with

F   81

more than the mind. You know, in your deepest awareness, the heart of the world, the home in which not only Truth and Beauty and Love abide but all of us. How then to you can life or any human being or Zen itself be 'cold?' It is you that have built that icy barrier about you, and it is the child of ignorance, illusion and the busy hands of self that would rob you of the greater life in which that self must die. As you know, I have faced the class again and again with Compassion as a theme for meditation and daily thought. It is all very well to prove that it is the twin of Wisdom, to give it philosophic basis and emotional support. But this won't do. Life begins when the flame of Bodhicitta, the Wisdom-heart, is born in a heart that sees now what an illusion is the world about us. When all that once gave pleasure is dust and ashes, and all that we gained seen as a piling up of sand that waits but the incoming tide, there *must* be a time of misery, the 'dark night of the soul' as the Christian mystics called it, between the old life and the new. Walk on, I can give no other help to you, walk on through the valley, for the hills will rise beyond. Not that there will then be pleasure. Pleasure will not for a long time be so pleasurable. There will instead be pain, insufferable pain, as one who sees for the first time something of that 'mighty sea of sorrow formed of the tears of men', and knows that he can do practically nothing about it. Jung talks somewhere of the bravery of the man who consciously withdraws the great part of his projections, and instead of blaming every thing and person under the sun for his own shortcomings, faces his own shadow and consumes it. But if it needs such courage to face our own troubles and deficiencies, how much greater the will, and large the heart, that can assume the sorrows of mankind. We cannot, but we are dedicated from that moment to work for the benefit of all mankind, and individual salvation or Nirvana becomes impossible. This is the dawn of the Bodhisattva, the dawn of true compassion, and the birth of a new worker to assist that body of Great Ones who labour mightily, untiringly, for the sake of all. In that great Brotherhood there is always room for recruits, with few great virtues, maybe, and plenty of faults and failings, but with the awakened heart of love for all that suffer and the will to relieve that suffering until that day when the last blade of grass shall enter into Enlightenment. Within that Brotherhood, even just inside the door, can there be talk of loneliness or of the coldness of humanity or the long night of sorrow, or of Zen? Fie on you! Get busy, for the work is heavy and the labourers are few.

Yours beside you,

LETTER 24

Dear Bungy,

Don't be so impatient. Of course you want what you call the advanced stuff, but have you learnt the early lessons yet? I doubt if I have and I've been at it twenty years longer than you (in this incarnation at any rate). You seem to be well integrated in the Western psychological sense, but are you yet integrated as between East and West, with your Western unconscious and all? Certainly many others in the class are not, and anyhow may I remind you that I am a schoolmaster and not a Zen master? The most I claim is to be the patient, humble trainer of potential raw material. In Ballet terms I teach the exercises at the barre for the training of muscle control, leaving the Master to teach 'entrechats dix' and the finer subtleties of Giselle.

As for the Class, first I must get my very mixed family to work as a whole. With ages from 20 to 70, both sexes, (did I hear you say 'at least?'? You shall be well beaten)—with education almost nil to University degrees, with scientists, artists, lawyers and psychologists mixed with civil servants, business men and housewives, with introverts and extraverts and all varieties of Jung's four groups, and every variety of Christian, Buddhist, Theosophist and Jew—what a chameleon is needed, and what am I? Much time must therefore be spent in working this mixture into an amalgam of one-pointed interest in Zen. They are now generally aware of the basic principles which must be well rubbed in before they can begin to move in the direction of Zen with any profit; they know that Zen is beyond the reach of thought, a whole time job and not an added activity, to be found within and in no book, teacher or God, that it is to be found by the intuition, can't be proved, and will not be achieved by being good or by metaphysical speculation. And so on. That it is not cold, or a new religion, or Japanese, and that it needs courage and guts galore, applied and long sustained, to find it. And that I am *not* a Zen Master . . .

All this is largely negative. What now? We need something more positive to begin. For the coming session, therefore, I shall turn them into themselves to answer, 'What do I want—Who wants—Why, and How?' Then what? I think a slow deepening of the search, not too fast lest the very effort produce its opposite, depressing when you think you are moving to the Light, or the More or whatever be your analogy. But if we press too hard we *are* pushed back again, and we have to move forward slowly, patiently, consolidating every foot of the way. We must not cease from walking on, but it is wise to live awhile in each new landscape we achieve. Meanwhile to the lazy I preach bloody warfare—to the violent, peace. It is better so. You think me a violent fellow. I am not, nor peaceful; my sole virtue is that I do walk on unceasingly, dragging the whole of me up the mountain path with blood and sweat but also with a savage joy and much unholy laughter. Well or ill, with gusto or with deep exhaustion, night and day weekends included I have walked, for forty years, in grim pursuit of my self-appointed task, my Dharma for this life. And it is this. The Buddha was a man who became the All-Enlightened One, the All-Compassionate One—in the words of a lesser Master of the Wisdom, 'the greatest as the holiest man that ever lived'. He taught the Way to that attainment, and to his Bhikkhus said, 'Go ye forth . . . proclaim the Doctrine glorious, for the benefit of all mankind, for the benefit of gods and men.' I found that way, and trod it far enough to see that it will lead to that end. So I began to proclaim it. I was 21 then, 58 now, and shall go on proclaiming it until I die. That is all. One day another will arise in the West who will be a master of that Wisdom, a master of Zen. Until then I teach what I know. I can do no more; I would not dare do less. And you? Don't wait for me. But love me a little at times. I shall have need of it.

Yours proclaimingly,

CHAPTER V

THE WAY OPENS

To Members of the Zen Class:

Now that the annual Summer School is over we can get down to a new year's work. As everything to do with Zen is in the mind I shall begin with asking you four questions. I do not mind what the answers are, and may not even ask you. *You* have to find the answers, for it is you that need to know them. The first is: What do you want? The second: Who wants? The third: Why? The fourth: Where are you looking? Which is much the same as: How do you expect to find?

The first is not easy. Do you want Zen, and if so have you any clear idea of what it is you want? You cannot find a needle in a haystack without some idea of the appearance of a needle. How much harder is it to find Zen which has no shape at all. Yet finding Zen is the result of a one-pointedness far finer than most of us can achieve, and behind that tool, or needle, or battering ram, according as we use it, is the whole strength of the will, the total power of the man. Think of a thousand-ton pressure behind a battering ram with the point of a needle, and you have some concept of the penetrating power needed, as I believe, to pierce through our present self-made barriers of ignorant thinking and clinging which bar us from the Light. Only when the whole of our energy is concentrated on the point so fine that it is but nominally there at all shall we succeed, and please do not infuriate me with foolish talk of 'No effort is needed. Just be natural, spontaneous and let go'. If that is so, why do you not do it? I will tell you. Because, as I have said a hundred times, it needs tremendous energy to let go, vast self-control to be spontaneous, tremendous will-power to be natural. Who do you know that has achieved it, and how long did it take them to achieve? I repeat, it needs great will-power to break through to Zen, though the technique used may be as simple as peeling potatoes all the live-long day.

If you are satisfied that you know what you want and that you truly and desperately want it, ask yourself the next question. I will allow you to be brilliant and tell me that all desire is the root of suffering and leads to no good when I am satisfied you have the guts to produce a real earth-shaking, heaven-quaking desire. I will then permit you to drop it! Meanwhile, *want*, as a man whose head is held under water wants air. That minutely directed want being assembled and rightly directed, ask yourself: Who wants? The answer is not the facile 'I'. *Who am I?* I am told that the late Maharshi of India, one of the greatest Masters of the Wisdom of modern times, would tell his pupils to ask themselves that question only, for if answered all else would be answered too. *What* I, at what level, so to speak, wants Zen? Your body, your emotions—to get an emotional kick out of the experience, with boasting to one's friends—the intellect, to discuss it proudly in terms of concept large and small, *who* wants? Your intuition? What is it, and is what it discovers *yours*? Do *you* know when the intuition speaks, or is there a flash of knowing? So who wants Zen? You know my 'working division' of the self, Self and SELF, for which I am so fiercely castigated by orthodox Theravadin Buddhists. They say there is no self of any kind or spelling. They may be right, but the Buddha did not say so, and their own favourite scripture, the Dhammapada, makes the distinction clear in a dozen places between Self and self. 'Self is the lord of self', it says, and surely this is obvious. There is the self you despise in you, the 'shadow' with which you must sooner or later come to terms; there is the Self, the best of you, that learns and grows and suffers and walks on to its own and the world's enlightenment. Is that all? How can it be? How can we gain Enlightenment if its seeds are not already within? How can there be change and becoming and the formed unless there is indeed an Unchanging, Formless Be-ness of which they are the shadow in the world we know? Call THAT what you will. For convenience, having no fear of names or concepts, I call it SELF. It *is*, but it is not yours or mine. *It* does not *want* Zen for it *is* Zen. What, then, *does*? Find out!

Why? Why seek for Zen? That is the third question, and it will soon prove fundamental. All work, reflecting our several types of introvert and extravert, is inward, for self-improvement, or outward, for the salvation of all mankind. The one type works in miniature, for the Self of one is the Self of all; the other works on the grand scale knowing that all which affects the whole must affect each part. But why we do what we do is of profound importance for it is the motive for any act which makes it 'right' or 'wrong', that is, helping or hindering the return to wholeness of all creation, the return of the many to the One, and of the One to that which is beyond all difference. Such is the flow of the cosmic tide; assist it and the selfish self is dissolved away, leaving unity, ('Forgoing self the Universe grows I'); hinder it and the obstacle is hurt and finally smashed by the relentless flow. So why do you want Zen? For your enlightenment, your pride? For the benefit of gods and men, as the Buddha sent his Bhikkhus forth to preach thə Dhamma? Or why? It is well to know.

The rest is a matter of technique but not to be despised. All achievement is achieved by method of some sort, all is done by some device or means to the chosen end. 'Skill in means' (*upaya-kausalya*) ranks as a tremendous virtue in Mahayana Buddhism, and the means can be as important as the end. (Later we may come to see that the means is indeed the end, and that the distinction is, like all else, falsely imagined). Meanwhile the wise man, having decided what of him wants what and why, is well advised to study how. Some plan of action, however fluid, saves waste of energy and leads the more swiftly to results.

Ask yourselves these questions, then, and see that they are answered. Then return to your complaints, on which you have, it seems, so much energy and time to spend that we do not get on faster. As one of you has truthfully announced to me, you get the teacher you deserve, and none better! This is my pace. Speed your own if you will and then come back to teach us. But remember one of the most truthful games invented—Snakes and Ladders . . .

Good hunting,

October 1958.   Christmas Humphreys,

87

LETTER 26

Dear Mary,

I apologise for saying that I am delighted to hear you are unhappy.
I have no envy for the allegedly happy. They are mostly fools
wandering vaguely in a fool's paradise. Of course the turmoil
of your new internal efforts makes you unhappy, or, rather, makes
you more aware of your basic unhappiness. So was the Buddha.
That is why he sought and found enlightenment. Hence Buddhism.
What is this happiness you have lost? A general, somewhat smug,
superficial (self)-satisfaction with circumstances. An apparently
stable condition of achievement. But it *must* be temporary, for *all*
is changing *all* the time, and the conditions which create that
happiness today will be gone tomorrow. And it is selfish because
it is blind to circumstances. You are better without it, for its
opposite, unhappiness, is the best of all spurs to right effort. When
you are sufficiently unhappy you look for a cure, which involves
looking for the cause of the unhappiness. Which is basic Buddhism.
For had the Buddha, as a young prince in his father's palace, been
content with the ingredients of happiness provided him, health,
wealth, beauty, a palace of beautiful women, friends and so on,
he would never have gone forth to find the cure for suffering and,
having found it, stayed on earth to offer it to all mankind.

Face it, as never before, that life is changing, that the thing we
call self is no exception and that our ignorance of these basic,
demonstrable facts is the cause of our suffering, for we strive
to live as if the opposite were true. The cause of suffering, then,
is our selfish desire, our craving to add to this unreal, unhappy,
miserable thing that struts and brags and strives to add to itself . . .
Put it in the dustbin and let's begin to live.

And even if you were 'happy' at some moment? What have you
wilfully forgotten, behind the high walls of your illusion? The
answer is all the rest of the forms of life, your brother the man
next door who is dying of cancer, your sister the tart on the streets
at night to earn money for a crippled younger brother (yes, those
stories are true at times), your child the rabbit in the trap, and the
millions of hopeless lovers, those who grieve for loved ones lost
and those who are bound, or so they seem, to hateful relatives,
employers and the burden of unnumbered days of hopeless, useless

living. And mentally? The utterly frustrated, the jeered at ugly, stupid ones, the frightened ones who see but penury ahead. Am I piling this on? I am, to help you see that *you* are to be envied, not the happy ones. You are free now to snap out of it, not back into happiness but into joy, untouchable, unshakeable, serene with open eyes and all awareness, working, working *happily* to dry one drop of that 'mighty sea of sorrow formed of the tears of men'.

Therefore I stand by what I wrote in my Pelican *Buddhism*, which was taken in turn from my *What is Buddhism?* which I wrote in 1926-7, (largely in the Temple, when I sat at my desk as the pupil of a famous barrister): 'The happiness which most men seek is a fool's paradise, a condition of self-inducement, illusion, a halting by the way-side to pluck the poisoned fruits of self, for it can only be obtained by ignoring the misery of our fellow men. Our very efforts to find happiness for ourselves prevent us finding it. True happiness is only to be found in ceaseless effort on behalf of suffering mankind'. And I quoted Shelley in Queen Mab:

> For when the power of imparting joy
> Is equal to the will, the human soul
> Requires no other heaven.

Whether you work to self-expansion or to self-forgetfulness is immaterial; these two ways, as I have often said, are complementary. But both involve facing the shadow of our baser selves, and will be rewarded with gleams of joy of an inner harmony and balanced, deep compassion for suffering in all its forms about us. Then we begin to ignore pleasure, pain, not failing to notice which is which, but caring less which it happens to be! You are going to the dentist and he will hurt you? He will hurt you. You are going to a show which you like? You will be pleased. So what? To the extent you like you will be unhappy if you can't go and that you dislike you will be pleased if you don't have to go. Either way you are fettered by your like-dislike. You will learn to rise above the domination of your admitted, accepted like-dislike. Do you see what I mean? Just *be* unhappy. Growl and grumble and complain to all and sundry, but get on with it, go through with it, take it on the jaw, then laugh and to hell with it! Enjoy what you like intensely, whether you should or shouldn't, and hate enormously and loudly.

But don't stop. The whole vast universe is but a turning wheel of ever-becoming, and all these trivial differences of the pairs of opposites are of no importance at all. It's raining hard, the telephone won't work, you have a cold and nobody loves you. So what? *Get on* with it, push its face in, yell with laughter and WALK ON!

Golly, what a letter, but I must get you out of this silly mood. How can you find Zen when you think it seriously matters if you *have* torn your mackintosh, lost your reading goggles and also your sense of the Eternal. Try a tin of Turkish Delight. I seem to remember it used to give you enormous happiness . . .

Unhappily yes, but yours joyfully,

LETTER 27

Dear Sally,

So you are another unhappy one. You'd better weep on Mary's shoulder now that you are such friends. She too is most unhappy, and not pleased at my saying Hurray. But I am quite firm on the matter. I should like to see 30 unhappy people in the class who (*a*) knew they were unhappy, (*b*) accepted that fact as quite right and proper and (*c*) were not therefore wasting time on trying to be happy. That to me would be excellent material for marching forward. When so much time is spent on trying to be happy there is little left for gaining happiness. For happiness, as you know perfectly well with your head and, I suspect your heart, comes from ceasing to seek anything for yourself and swimming happily with the tide of the Great Cosmic Purpose (most Victorian) to the inward peace which is the fruit of ceasing to seek anything at all. Yes, even Zen, for the seeking is itself a dual state of mind—*I* want *that*—which is two things, when there is only one in Reality. So *be* unhappy. Even as you have as an artist learned to look at things until you become them, so seek Zen without seeking it. Just become it.

Incidentally you raise another point, that you cannot in meditation look at anything without wanting to draw it or paint it or do something about it. All right. Listen. Listen as hard as you usually look. I noticed the other day when you put on a Bach Chorale you were wandering round the Studio humming the tune but not giving it your whole or even half your attention. Now put it on again.

90

Sit back and relax utterly. Become all ears, and follow the sound completely. Flow in it, surge with it, fall with it, become it. Use your whole will to be there, in it, and with it, and at the end fall back as if exhausted with the glory, the emotion, the excitement and the joy of it. You will have ceased to be for a while and that is Zen— or as near as damn it, as our old gardener used to say. Incidentally, the exercise will make you happy again, but not with happiness . . .

Yours choralically,

LETTER 28

To Members of the Zen Class.

Your reaction to my last letter a month ago has been so violent that I must answer the answers collectively.

So far in the present course we have laid foundations, partly negative, clearing away rubbish, and partly positive, laying new foundations. I have adopted the Eastern technique of teaching, by approaching the same subject by a score of different directions instead of a single step by step approach from one. In terms of painting I have marked out a large canvas, with a picture (painfully dim at times) in my mind, and then I paint it by touches, seemingly unrelated here and there, a sketch in this corner, an area of red in another, two superimposed and contrary drawings in the middle and so on—very bad art (save by the most modern methods of technique) but the result, for some of you, would seem to be successful, to build up a picture of the Thing in the Middle which, if you stand well back, conveys, that is the word, an impression of my understanding to you. By using a vast variety of concept and emotion one may avoid the evils of concept, that it shuts up the flight of the mind in a box, and that it binds in the world of duality THAT which is not.

So now we can look at our individual and collective progress, all of which takes place of course within. I see the vast majority of your minds and means of progress in San-zen; you see the great variety of types as you sit in class; the larger unit is a unit of humanity. And I see facets of myself in all your failings and findings, and grow with you, though not, I think at times, as fast as some of you.

Now let us consider Direct action, not because I want to at the moment, but there is a peevish, impatient spirit abroad, as hounds on the leash that wish to be let go after the fox of Zen. But note this, that direct action is an attitude of mind and not a choice of subject or object. Let us suppose I arrive at the platform to find my train just leaving, and there is an hour to wait for the next. Here is a situation to be faced, as all others, directly or indirectly. I can allow emotions to surge through my mind—annoyance, regret I did not leave sooner, fear of the consequences of missing the appointment. Or (and possibly *and*) I can project my feelings onto objects around, by cursing the porter, kicking my bag when it falls off the seat, hurling mental blame on the railway company, the weather, my taxi driver and so on. Or I can face the situation and *accept* it. I have an hour, an empty hour. But how wonderful! What a chance to take exercise and breathe fresh air, to make notes for that lecture, to meditate in the waiting room or walking up and down! That, as I see it, is direct action, a direct adjustment of the mind to the circumstance as it is, whatever it is, without erecting a mass of concepts, emotion and the like between self and circumstance. It may be direct action to sit with hands in lap, doing nothing, if it is a convenient opportunity for that most refreshing experience. So please get out of the attitude that I am to throw you objects for direct action, like stones for a dog to pursue and bring back. Things and events and situations and people are all about you. Tackle all of them *directly*; why wait for me? So let it be more direct by all means, but get on with it, all of you, each of you, now, here, and with this!

Yours directly,
Christmas Humphreys.
November 1958.

LETTER 29

Dear Silver,

I am sorry that the bars of thought, though thinner, are still there. Don't you want to get out? You will agree that Zen is Zen. Well? How then can it be 'a mysticism of the will'? All right, I used that phrase myself, but I can learn, and I soon gave up trying to understand A by describing it in terms of B. A bus is a bus. Why then go out of your way to call it a Roman chariot with four wheels and driven by an internal combustion engine instead of a horse? Don't even call it a bus. Get in, pay your fare, get out and forget it. To misquote the poet, 'Seek thou me for what I am—So shalt thou find me fairest'. You see, you are under the illusion that by describing —which means confining in concepts—something you do not know in terms of something you do know, you learn—but learn what? More *about* it! But that is not the road to Zen. Let me repeat for the thousandth time, Zen is not about anything, and nothing will help you that is only about Zen. You must take Bodhidharma's formula au pied de la lettre—'a direct seeing into the heart of man', not more and more *about* it. Go for it. Don't ask a friend to hold the rabbit for you while you shoot it with your little bow and arrow. Shoot! You are guilty of the refinement of an execution by shooting, when they hang a target over the man's heart. Only when you shoot Zen in the heart unaided, will you—not Zen—fall dead.

Have another go.

Good Shooting,

T.

LETTER 30

Dear Martha,

So psychic visions are flashing merrily. No matter, so long as they do not have the devastating effect of making you pause to look at them. Walk on, and let them flash. But your question about emotion and the intuition needs thoughtful answering. Can emotion lift to a point when the intuition floods it with light as it does with very high thinking? That, I think, is what you are after. Why not? I have no authority for my answer, so I use, when in doubt, my own reason and experience. Why not, I repeat, for the complex 'self' is not in fact, as we talk of it, laminated or built as a seven storey house. The skins of an onion is a better analogy, but an onion in which the interrelations of the different parts are inconceivably complex, subtle, fascinating and complete. The finest or subtlest or nearest the centre, or that with the finest matter for form, is the intuition (for Atman is not yours or mine). It potentially irradiates, as I see it, any other 'part' of the total man, thought, feeling, the senses and all else. Indeed Bhakti Yoga, that form of Yoga which uses the emotions at their finest, being the love-devotion to the Ideal in this form or another, reaches great heights with pure

93

devotion, unsullied with self. Mary is an introvert bhakti type, and extremely intuitive.

Indeed most mystics are intuitive-emotional, and the intellectual mystic is less common. Eckhart is, I suppose, the supreme example of the latter, for his intuitive awareness is only equalled by the dazzling brilliance of his metaphysics. Only Suzuki that I know today talks on the same plane, and it is interesting that he is a great student of Eckhart. But most of the Christian mystics, and the Persians that I have read, are more bhakti, like you. But lest you feel contented (the most loathsome condition known to man) let me add that you have still to develop your intellect, and to the full, before you achieve, or even before you are accepted as a member of the Goal-Winners Club whose clubhouse is on the higher slopes of Zeneverest. Carry on, and if you flaunt your psychic powers at me I shall turn on mine and haunt you in the night!

Yours emotionally,

LETTER 31

Dear Mary,

I am sorry if I did not make myself clear on the subject of happiness. Of course it is better than unhappiness, and of course I do not despise or derogate joy. Joy is a flame, a warm and self-consuming fire, for in it we are more than we. It is expansive, and embraces an enormous field about us. We want to sing and dance and hug everything about us. Why? Because we feel one with them and love them all. But this I think is a child of Prajna, a reaction to an awareness beyond emotion or feeble happiness. Contentment can be to other temperaments much the same. It is the negative, perhaps, of Joy, Joy's quieter sister, but just as beautiful. It is the serenity of a level line, no longer the rough waves of *samsara* but the still pool of a higher consciousness. Steady, because the winds pass through it as through spring flowers on an April day; the mind is unaffected by any circumstances for it does not react to its importunity. Taking all things as they come, it slaps no labels on them. Receiving thoughts and messages, it blows a kiss to them and lets them by. But heavens, what a long Way away from the thing we crave for and call happiness!

Yours joyfully,

94

LETTER 32

Dear Sally,

Don't worry about your depression. Just be depressed. You remember the story of the Indian King who ordered his jeweller to make him a ring on which would be engraved a sentence which would cheer him in depression and deflate him in undue delight. The jeweller returned with a ring on which was engraved, 'It will pass'. We hung that in our dug-out during the bombing of London. As a useful application of the doctrine of *anicca*, change, it worked well.

You see, many an artist works on a cycle of inspiration. There are heights and there must be depths, and perhaps the bumps are proportionate to the heights attained. At your best you paint or engrave or model nothing at all. You get out of the way and let painting or engraving or modelling happen. You criticise objectively afterwards and make technical improvements (sometimes spoiling it thereby). The creative principle, or rhythm of life is in you but not of you; in your great moments you 'attach your belt to the power-house of the Universe', as Trine put it. The medium used is immaterial, a picture, a dance, a speech or a book, and *your* appraisal alone matters. You will cease to care what others, save fellow artists perhaps, think of your work. *You* will know if it is good or bad, and others' praise or violent blame will unaffect you. But I said 'appraisal', which is not self-appraisal (sorry). Remember the Voice of the Silence: 'Self gratulation, O Lanoo, is like unto a lofty tower up which a haughty fool has climbed. Thereon he sits in prideful solitude, and unperceived by any but himself.' I like that. Self-appraisal is different, and the inner content of a job well done is, subject to slapping it on the head if it begins to grow, a nice experience.

So your depression will pass, and be replaced with creative activity. And that mood will pass . . . So it goes on. Walk on, for satori is beyond that cycle, and is steady as a flame that glows in a windless place. We shall reach it.

My love to you, creatively,

LETTER 33

Dear Bungy,

Forgive me for saying so but you seem to be getting a wee bit smug over your 'balance' and 'poise' and no problems. We all have problems and none of us is truly balanced yet, nor will be till Enlightenment, when the factors making for unbalance are removed. Even if you were as poised as you seem to think, you are spoiling it with pride, which is self again, which is unbalance. There is a social class analogy which comes to me. The working classes are uninhibited in their knowledge and acceptance of what they are. The middle class reach upward, and their terribly careful conduct is inhibited all the time with fear lest they slip down a rung of the ladder. The upper classes have no such fear, and can afford to be uninhibited once more. Are you possibly clinging a little tightly to your freedom and poise? If so, you have not really got it.

I am receiving 'rave' notices about *Zen Buddhism* in its new edition, but do not allow myself to forget Dr Suzuki's own comment. On seeing the first copy he sighed and said, 'I suppose you in the West *have* to be so intellectual!' But I think it most unfair that people should write and say they had the most *marvellous* experiences after reading it, when the poor author didn't when writing it! Meanwhile, the following seems pertinent.

Asked a new member, riven with doubt,
'Just what is this book all about?
    Why write at such length
    With such *wabi* and strength
If the goose in the bottle is out?'

'Your bewilderment can't be denied,'
The *satoric* author replied.
    'But how can the goose
    Be at last on the loose
Unless all the time it's inside?'

Yours fatuously,

LETTER 34

Dear Silver,

Let's get this matter of tolerance and intolerance clear. You say you are quite prepared to let the other fellow go to hell his own way. Let's analyse that. It implies that you are quite convinced he is going to hell, i.e. on the wrong road, and that you will graciously permit him to proceed. But how are you so *certain* he is on the wrong road, for him, at this moment, in his present condition and state of development? Even wandering down a blind alley may be right at times if there is no other way of making quite sure it is a blind alley. Look again at the definition of tolerance I took from Annie Besant long ago—'an eager and a glad acceptance of the way along which others seek the Truth'. Eager and glad acceptance— that's positive, not sneering, an actual aid to *their* progress on *that* way. If you had a godson who was clearly 'called' to the Church, would you not actively help him to enter it? If not, why not? It would not be right for *you*, *now*, but if it is clearly what *he* wants and would be useful and happy in, why hinder him—*why not help*?

Only such an attitude makes true co-operation possible. Co-operation implies the free and willing working together of free units, having mutual respect. From individuals lift the level to schools. Take the Buddhist organisations in London. *How* should they co-operate, assuming, as is obvious, that they should? Surely with an eager and glad acceptance of the way the other one proclaims and teaches Buddhism? We cannot and should not all be the same, but we must genuinely admit that the others are doing what they think right and doing it their way, and that they *may* be right. At the same time we must leave them to be different and not even work for a synthesis which pleases no one, still less for a compromise which would be worse. Cannot one of them teach Theravada, another Mahayana, another a specific method of meditation and another indulge in Tibetan ritual? Why not? Why not leave each free to go its own way, meeting as friends and colleagues and fellow Buddhists? But you want to decide once and for all which is right, and then force the dissenters into the path chosen by the majority. What impertinence, what arrogance to think that any decision should be made, and that if made it could be right to force the others into that majority way. We aren't members of a parish

G   97

council deciding where to put the new Memorial Hall, but pilgrims on an age-long road to self-Enlightenment. As such we walk alone, but hand in hand, for heaven knows we need each other's help in the darkness of our common ignorance.

How could I do what you seem to expect me to do in our Class and force everyone to go the same way? Even if I produced the insufferable conceit to attempt it? Have you any conception of the variety of minds in that group, even apart from the obvious differences of sex, and age and education? The introvert and extravert need totally different handling. The intellectuals and the emotional or feeling type, ditto. The natural mystics versus the natural occultists or ritualists or magicians or spiritual scientists, call them what you will. And the Karma yogins, those working by right action, who want to know all the time what to *do*, they should be allowed to do a hundred different things in as many ways. None of these is right or wrong, but probably right for that person at that time and place and that stage of development. Is there a Zen type? Yes and no; not a type but a frame of mind. Zen is a technique for transcending the duality of thinking and thus to achieve a 'moment' of satori, which is Non-duality—and therefore utterly beyond thought. Who shall dogmatise and say that A or B or C should best approach this 'moment' in this or that particular way? Not I. My job is to help each on his road to that end, to guide as I may, but with suggestions only. To suggest, but never to command, and always to know, genuinely, that in anything I say I may be wrong—for that person at that time, in the advice I give. Think this over, for the germ of intolerance once settled in is hard to remove, and we must remove it.

Yours, tolerant of all save intolerance,

LETTER 35

Dear Mr Crashaw,

Don't apologise for asking questions, and please bring them up in Class. It is the stimulating effect of the new minds of new members, so to speak, which prevents us stagnating in a dull contentment. Your present question is difficult to answer precisely—What has Zen got that the Western mystics haven't got? I think the answer is *something*, but it may be more in technique of achievement than what is achieved. First, however, is the fact that Zen is a school for the achievement of its goal, with a line of teachers and pupils. I know of no Western school of mysticism for the development of the faculty of the intuition by which that mystical experience is attained. Few in the world have attained higher than Eckhart, but he taught none and none followed him; he merely sought to preach what he had found to be true, which is not the same thing at all.

The technique is of course enormously different, and as I see it springs from a different temperament. The Western mystic was largely *bhakti* yoga, that is, of the devotional type—Jung would probably classify them as introvert intuitive-emotional. This is a far cry from the rumbustious, laughing, strenuous, beyond-thought-striving youngster of a Zen monastery. But it is difficult indeed to convey the flavour or perfume of Zen effort as found in Japan; certainly it is very different from the equivalent flavour I find in the writings of recognised mystics, whether European, Persian or Indian. Most of these were *bhakti* yogis, as I have said, or metaphysical in their approach to bursting through into the thing in itself, the *tathata* or suchness of things, via the higher realms of thought. The Zen man is unique in his approach, ever direct yet exquisitely balanced on the median line, roaring with laughter while deadly serious, scorning all abstractions and high-sounding phrases, with no formulated Ideal, still less a personified Saviour or God, fighting with self to get to No-self, with thought to attain No-thought, striving to break all forms in order to remain Whole, humbly-proud—he is a man *sui generis*, and either you long to be like him, to work with him, or you do not like him at all.

But to be practical, I see no difficulty in answering your question. The mystical type is as clear and easily distinguishable as the scientist or the artist. You are or are not of that type—I think you are not. Whether you are the Zen type is for you to say—I think you are. But first you must have courage to take the plunge. You are standing on the edge, wondering how cold the water is. That way you will not get wet, and Zen is the water.

Here's to good diving,

LETTER 36

Dear Bungy,

We seemed to be all tangled up the other night on Gurus, masters, leaders and me. Let's get it clear. The immemorial method of the East is the Guru-chela relationship, which is highly personal, largely on a devotional basis, with complete freedom, however, for the pupil to move to another teacher after due 'notice'; and the teaching is graded by the teacher to the power of the pupil to assimilate. This is the real meaning of esoteric; it is not that the master refuses to teach anything he knows, but you do not attempt to teach the Integral Calculus to a child of ten, and you do not hand on the guarded secrets of, say, occult forces of the mind, until the pupil is ready to develop those forces in his own mind, *and to use them wisely and unselfishly*. The Zen technique is enormously different. It is assumed that the pupil knows that the Absolute Itself is to be found within, and that no man or God can give a man what he has not got. The job is how to help the pupil break his self-created bonds and so be free, how to help him to know that he is already enlightened, how to 'see' things, his self and the relationship of all of them, *as they are*. The nearest Western equivalent is the psychiatrist, who is trained so that his own views and personality shall interfere to the minimum with his objective analysis of the patient's mind. He holds up a mirror; it is for the patient to see in it his own complexes, barriers, kinks and lopsidedness. Of course the ideal teacher or master is at once priest, doctor, teacher and loving friend. But he must be impersonal, must have some intuitive powers to see the pupil-patient's needs, and be immensely patient. For the rest, he can but lead the pupil to his own level, and push him a little beyond. Then the pupil seeks another master, one who knows more than he or can help him further, and there is no emotional reaction in any direction at the change. In a class, the pupils should be 'as the fingers of one hand', and any personal dislike, jealousy, envy or any other disturbing emotion between them weakens the group as such and makes the teacher's job more difficult. Is this clearer? I repeat, to be personal, 'Judge thou me by what I am. So shalt thou find me fairest.' I am, as one of you so rightly said, the teacher you deserve. Deserve a better, find him, and move on, (if he or she will have you).

Meanwhile to work, as I must that I may the better teach.
With love,

LETTER 37

Dear Silver,

Do keep your eye on the ball, which is Zen. You are like a small child at the dentist; let's talk about the cat or the pictures on the wall, anything rather than have that tooth out. What do these distinctions matter? If you want Zen go for it, single- and whole-heartedly. Surely you can answer your question for yourself, but here is mine. You want to know the distinction between intuitive inspiration and the spiritualist's 'voices'. The answer is that the Self is inconceivably complex, and you in your medicine deal with but the body and a vague and comparatively new discovery called the mind. The relationship between the parts of the whole are so elaborate no chart could include them, and all our talk of planes and faculties is futile if it claims completeness. It has its uses, however, and we must use some such analogy. Zen experience, then, comes from the Prajna plane through Buddhi, the intuition. It is quite unmistakable and he who asks if this is satori is answered. If there is doubt it isn't! But there can clearly be flashes of intuition short of satori, illumining intellectual understanding, (and perhaps emotional too). There are also intellectual 'jumps', when things suddenly click into place. Buddhi is helping here. But psychic 'hunches', visions, etc. are of a different order, and pertain to the psychic plane. In terms of my lighthouse, the psychic, or astral plane is the third up; above it is the mind as thinking machine, concrete and abstract, then Buddhi. Buddhi *knows*; the psychic awareness is almost always wrong, being mirror-wise to this plane, of substance finer and less fixed; and the eyes with which we see it, and use clairvoyance, are only opened to see clearly on that plane by long training. There are psychics in thousands, and whole nations have 'the sight' in their peasants still, but how many trained and reliable psychics does one know? A dozen? You are fortunate!

And so to spiritualism. To the extent that this involves a human medium going negative and letting some discarnate entity speak or write through the deserted vehicles, it is unnatural and utterly evil. That is the unanimous voice of the 'white' or true Teachers of all religions and schools of the Wisdom since the world began. The practice is as old as man, but no better for that. From the crudest Voodoo to the Oracles of classic antiquity, from Madam See-all in a Mayfair flat to Bön Tibetan performances, all this is unnatural, contrary to nature, and at our stage of evolution utterly and horribly wrong. It is more, it is dirty, as those who grub in the dust-bin, and it causes grave damage to all three entities concerned. I know what I am saying, being somewhat psychic. I have seen the appalling inner condition of the medium, the degradation of morale, and I know the difficulties of helping those who, from the practice in this life or in past lives have lost control of their own vehicles and just slide out at the will of anything, living or discarnate, that wishes to take control. This, of course, is profoundly different from the willing surrender of one's 'bodies' to the use of a higher mind. But the pupil so trained is extremely rare, and the adept who can use such a person is far rarer. One of the most famous in modern times was H. P. Blavatsky, who consciously lent herself as the amanuensis, to some extent, of her Master Morya. But here is the vast distinction; she was conscious all the time, and knew precisely what she was writing. For her it was no more than telepathic dictation. The negative medium, on the other hand, has no knowledge of what has been happening when she was 'out of the body'.

The evil wrought? To the medium; she loses control of herself so often that she ceases to have the power to prevent herself being pushed out by this and that of the many entities which crowd the psychic plane. The Self as a unit disintegrates and with it her morale. Some keep control of themselves, most don't, and the living entity that uses such a medium pushes her down into the mud each use, like using a prostitute. More, the user of the medium relies more and more on the 'messages' thus received, and the reliance on the Light within grows steadily weaker. Surrender to this un-spiritual control makes self-reliance more difficult, and such practice is most unspiritual and utterly non-Zen.

But that is not all. There is the invading entity to consider. It may be a hungry *preta*, or ghost, the disintegrating remnants of a human being, an elemental or some other non-human entity. If human, it is not the man we knew. He has passed on, on the karmic tide, and if he has not, but is held as a fly in a web by the machinations of these black magicians, then his evolution is delayed and affected by his being drawn back into the vortex. And what does 'he' teach or say or write? Nothing of spiritual value, and generally speaking not one word new that was not already in the brain of the deceased. These shreds of clothing should be allowed to vanish utterly, leaving the man with his karmic complex of forces to move on, still learning, till he is drawn back to incarnation by the force of that self's desire. What a revolting picture it all is, and how the cultured Eastern mind marvels and is disgusted to see the intelligentsia of the West assembled round the dust-bin, or worse, the graveyard, to dabble with this evil-smelling refuse of the 'dear departed'.

So choose, a clean climbing to the Light, using the immemorial Wisdom offered you, or 'voices' from a stinking graveyard, saying nothing at all. There is no compromise.

Yours fiercely, from experience,

LETTER 38

Dear Mary,

Don't apologise for talking of the Self and Atman and the One Self within. Why not? It is just as true as talking of the not-self and the not-Self and 'there is no self of any kind'. The difference seems to be to me one of emphasis and technique. I find the Theravadin insistence on no-self extremely dreary, and have found it so since I first read it forty years ago. By all means learn with care and force that the self we call 'I' is nothing but a bundle of illusion, and ram that fact well into yourself. But there is, of course, SELF, as the Pali scriptures admit, though many of the modern pundits hate to be reminded of it. If there were not an Uncreated, Unformed, Unmade, how could there be, as there is, a created, formed and made world of *samsara*, of the everyday? And I claim a Self as well! (I am told there was a heretical sect of Pudgalavadins who believed in Self—I wish to revive it). It is a good name for the thing which goes on from life to life, learning and purifying and expanding to Enlightenment. Call it Little Willy if you like, but you've got to call it something. But get this into your curly head. That if you prefer the positive approach, as more fun and joy and warmth and help to you, that all is SELF and in all forms we see the ONE SELF, know this, *that is just as wrong*. It is also one-sided, as the other is one-sided and therefore incomplete. Truth lies in the middle.

Yours Self-ishly,

LETTER 39

Dear Billy,

What to study? There I can help you, though I do not dictate. Zen is a school of 'direct transmission' of Enlightenment. As such it has no scriptures of its own, and no sermons of even the greatest of its Masters which, as intellectual doctrine, *must* be accepted. It uses many scriptures, in particular the Diamond Sutra and the Heart Sutra, which you will find together in Conze's *Buddhist Wisdom Books*, with commentary. The Lankavatara Sutra is enormous and you will find Dr Suzuki's *Studies in the Lankavatara* Sutra worth reading before you tackle his translation of the text itself. *The Sutra of Wei Lang* (*Hui Neng*) is easier reading and to many of us almost sufficient, but the lately published *Zen Teaching of Huang Po*, translated by John Blofeld, is a worthy brother to it. But I say read anything that stimulates intuition. Some books just ring a bell as soon as you open them; others interest the intellect but leave that bell unrung. If asked to choose a few in addition to the above I would add, first, the *Tao Tê Ching*, because it is often described as the mother of Zen Buddhism (the fierce Bodhidharma being the father, of course). Then I would add *The Voice of the Silence*, translated by H. P. Blavatsky, described by the late Anagarika Dharmapala, the greatest Buddhist missionary of modern times, as 'a pure Buddhist work' (I got my copy signed by the Dalai Lama when I knelt at his feet in Delhi). Then the *Bhagavad Gita*, in some ways the greatest scripture in the world. *The Dhammapada*, the fourth Gospel, Eckhart and, though lower in level, Marcus Aurelius and Epictetus. I would add, perhaps with a faint blush. Omar Khayyam, for there is great stuff in it as well as great beauty. And of modern works perhaps the best work Dr Suzuki ever wrote, at any rate for its size, his *Introduction to Zen Buddhism*. And finally, my own personal 'Bible', the section in the *Mahatma Letters to A. P. Sinnett* on Probation and Chelaship.

But this is a purely personal selection, and need not trouble you.

But note that none of these works is in any sense authority for the truth of anything in it. *You* must find Truth, and find it where you will, in the *Daily Mail*, the Bible, or the advertisements in *Punch*. If the statement appeals to your intuition as true, what does it matter who said it or where you found it? Your job is to study, not in the sense of reading through the book, but as you do one of your text-books, digesting, learning, annotating and comparing. Then give yourself time to digest; then read it again. May I close with a quotation from those Mahatma Letters (p. 262). 'Knowledge for the mind, like food for the body, is intended to feed and help growth, but it requires to be well-digested, and the more thoroughly the process is carried out the better both for body and mind'.

Good studying,

LETTER 40

Dear Rodney,

Watch that motive. It is easy in the enthusiasm of seeking for Zen to forget the purpose of the search. There is only one right motive, if one must have one, and that is Enlightenment, and not enlightenment for *you*. Still less enlightenment that you may proudly wear it as a new and dazzling headdress and flaunt with revolting pride at all your friends. It has been said that it is always right to seek self-knowledge but that it must be for the sake of the knowledge and not for self. For the Light you seek is not your Light, nor will it ever become yours. I know that you are keen to save the world, that you see yourself as a dedicated Bodhisattava living to that end. Very well, set to work and save it, but don't forget that one way to begin is by the elimination of the self in your own striving. May I quote your own favourite book for you, the Mahatma Letters? You probably know the passage, as I do, by heart, on page 252. It is the Master M. writing to Sinnett about the purpose with which men join the Theosophical Society. 'I say again then. It is he alone who has the love of humanity at heart, who is capable of grasping thoroughly the idea of a regenerating practical Brotherhood, who is entitled to the possession of our secrets. He alone, such a man— will never misuse his powers, as there will be no fear that he should turn them to selfish ends. A man who places not the good of man-

kind above his own good is not worthy of becoming our *chela*—
he is not worthy of becoming higher in knowledge than his neighbour . . .'

So watch that you don't spoil your fine ideals and genuine will
to serve humanity with private reservations about the glory in wait
for the Saviour!

Good saving,

LETTER 41

Dear Sally,

I agree with you that art can be largely a matter of the emotions
as the driving force, rather than the intellect, but don't take that
too far. Some of the greatest artists, using that term widely, have
been mighty minds, and some art can be very largely 'cerebral'
and none the worse for it. But I agree that intuition can illumine
the emotions in their production of inspired craftsmanship, and
that satori can be approached and indeed gained at a work-bench
or at the easel as easily as in purely intellectual pursuits. Indeed,
the history of the Zen masters shows pupils getting it during the
most menial occupations, or, as it were, by the accidental noise
of a spade against a stone. Meanwhile I hope you distinguish thought
from emotion. Any tool will do, or faculty, but it is well to know
what you are using, what colour and what brush, or what tool
at the bench. I get fierce when I hear people talk of giving a problem
'anxious thought'. There should be no such thing. If the clear
light of thought is clouded with anxiety, which is the emotion of
fear, there will be no clear solution to the problem. Think or feel
but don't mix them!

Yours aye,

LETTER 42

Dear Letchworth,

Don't apologise for criticism; it is the way I learn my job. If as a
new member of the group you find too much slick cleverness of
reply and comment, you show your perspicacity. There is. It is,
however, a necessary fault in pursuit of a great virtue. Zen lies on an
incredibly narrow way and on the non-existent middle of it. We

have to lighten our thinking, as it were, speed it up enormously, and then jump—not to conclusions or decisions, but to direct 'seeing' into the heart of things and of man. This direction of answer and comment must come 'suddenly' and immediately out of the mind—out of the unconscious, say some, and thought must intervene, at first, as little as possible. The leap of an answer is stimulated, so to say, by rapid thought, and thought which may deliberately leap to the opposite reply of the last speaker. Do you see what I mean? If one of us gives an answer that is good but still sense, and another caps it with a remark which is nonsense, this may be just quick, slick thinking, but it may come from an intuitive vision of the thing as one, and an expression of the other half of the first fellow's remark. The difference between clever-clever talk and the appearance of a real awareness is desperately fine, and I do not guarantee to be right in my diagnosis every time. Especially as sometimes my own remark is only, as I see at once when I have made it, clever-clever like the rest. We are shooting at a target a million miles away with a child's bow and arrow—and we shall miss many times (*pace* Mr Herrigel who learnt how to do it). But now and again we hit, and the bell rings and it was all well worth it. Read Blyth's *Zen in English Literature*, and you will see his hundreds of illustrations as to what is and what is not Zen in his quotations. Don't take what he says as gospel, even though he did spend 16 years in Zen monasteries in Korea. Make your own decisions; for myself I think that he is sometimes wrong. The line is so finely drawn between false and true that it is difficult to be sure how it falls. So I will agree with you that there is some and even much of the clever-clever in our talk, but please help us to reduce it by the true article. We shall know it when it comes.

Sincerely,

LETTER 43

Dear Silver,

Of course I don't mind criticism; I more than welcome it. Here I agree that it is well laid, for I used the word initiation too lightly, and without explanation. I meant no more than the stage at which that individual had reached in the College of Life, moving to a higher form. The One Initiator, as referred to in some manuals of the inner life is, like all else, within, and there is no one in gorgeous robes to hand a pass-word or a golden key to the successful candidate. But there *is* knowledge which is not given to those who have not proved themselves worthy to possess it safely and to use it wisely. The higher ranks of the 'Black-belts' of Judo in Japan, for example, have secret methods of killing, and of reviving, which are kept to themselves, and *they* make no claim to be an occult school of wisdom.

But the general right to criticism is most important. I am not fooling when I frequently say to the Class that I long to be rid of them collectively and individually. For a long time the pupil leans heavily on the teacher, and psychologically can get fixed in that attitude. The teacher's job is partly to put him on his feet again, to help him gain his release from such fixation on himself as the Guru, Father-Image etc. Indeed, until the pupil can without emotion or apology knock over the teacher's tea-bowl and laughingly walk out of the room he is not 'freed' of the teacher, and is still bound to his pupilage. Therefore the teacher rejoices whenever a pupil, from 'adoring' him and lapping up all he says *au pied de la lettre*, suddenly stands up and says 'Bosh' to a pronouncement with which he does not immediately agree. That behaviour, so far from being rude in the teacher's eyes, is a symptom of development. The yes-man has become an occasional no-man, and he is beginning to spread his wings. This does not mean that I am wrong and the critic is more right; it means that the critic accepts what he accepts as being found to be true, and will not accept it otherwise, which is a vast improvement. So argue as you will. All that I ask is that modicum of modesty which allows that I *may* be right even if you do not immediately see that I am. I in turn am modest enough to know that it is more than possible that I am wrong.

Lots more initiations,

LETTER 44

Dear Brampton,

You have indeed made marvellous progress in the last six months, but you still remind me of a man climbing a mountain in diver's boots and with enough furniture to supply a cottage tied round him. Your job at the moment is to 'Drop it'. If you do not know the story of that phrase let me tell it you. A venerable sage approached the Buddha, bearing flowers in either hand. 'Drop it', said the Blessed One. The sage dropped one of the bunches of flowers and came further. 'Drop it', came the order again. The sage obediently dropped the other flowers and still advanced. 'Drop it', came the final order. The Sage stopped, puzzled. 'Bring nothing', said the All-Seeing One. 'Come empty-handed'. Smiling the Sage obeyed, for in a flash of enlightenment he dropped and did not again pick up the self, which had so long stood as a dark wall between his eyes and his Enlightenment.

You too must drop these barriers; then only will you see. Used as a device almost anything may be useful, but when you do not even appreciate the load you carry, the burden is more than any man can take with him to the heights of Everest. What I am asking you to drop is not a device or anything useful but things that are dead, old views, opinions, values, thoughts. You know the loveliest phrase in all Buddhism. 'Let the mind alight nowhere'. Study it, absorb it, try it out. Leave space in the garden of your mind for the joy of direct experience, for the song of the wind on the heath, for the swoop and whirl and splendour of joy on the wing. (You *can't* be poetic with a diver's boots on). Study by all means, for the facts and ideas you cull from books are the raw material of fresh experience. But these thoughts of others are dead until your intuition lights them again to life. You must recreate what another is describing and so make it live.

As for what you drop, the answer in the end is everything. Meanwhile make a beginning by realising what you carry. First, the body, its likes and dislikes in food and comfort and temperature and clothes. Why be laden with the demands of eleven stone of mud? Your feelings. Be damned to them and put them in the dust-bin. Whose feelings? Yours? *What* you is hurt by *what*? What is hurt is pride, ambition, sense of self-importance. What are they doing inside you anyway? Your fears—whose? Frightened of what? Write it down and face it. Of growing old—you will. Of death—it must come. Your likes and dislikes—how many of these are of unimportant, evanescent trivialities? Yet the mind is even more cluttered up with rubbish, and the brilliant discovery of today may be the rubbish of tomorrow. No thought is of value save when it is 'working' as yeast in the mind; after that it is best discarded.

This applies to all opinions, political, social, or in your case horti-cultural. Remember that a 'conclusion' is something shut up, there-fore out of the flow of the river of life and on a sand-bank, dead, forgotten. Open it again and reconsider it. Principles and con-victions should be dusted and revised every first of the month. You will be surprised how lightly you tread on the second, like wearing slippers after a spell of gum-boots in the garden. Your duty, you say. Is it, or is it still? Out with it, into the dust-bin. Even your ideals—here is an interesting point I picked up in class last week. Either you and your end, or goal or ideal, are both free or both fixed. If you fix your *end*, immediate or ultimate, you fix yourself at the other end of the line. *You* are pinned down by your pinning down of the other end of your desire or endeavour. But the man with no more on his back than the next thing to be done, here and now and with this, is then free, as he was before, to walk on, whither he pleases.

But all that we carry is conditioned by habits of body and feelings and mind, and these habits are devils to be fought and vanquished. We must make new ones, like digging new trenches for a stream, *and* be able to fill them up again. The habit of labelling all things as good or bad, or liked or disliked, or interfering in others' affairs, of wishing 'if only' this and that would happen then all would be well—what folly! It would not, for we should still be much the same. Our habit of uncontrolled reaction to stimulus, from an advertisement which makes us buy something we don't want to an expression of annoyance when a person or event is mentioned. How we dissipate our energy in these reactions. Roars of delight, snarls of revenge, cold fear of consequences, hot anger (because someone parks his car outside your door)—what energy, what energy to think you can waste with impunity and still live to old age!

But enough, for you see the principle. We are so heavy laden, compared with the swallow, the naked baby, or for that matter the tramp. But our heaviest burdens are in the mind. In this I favour the old Zen story of the two monks at the ford. They were coming back at eventide to their monastery, and at a ford saw a pretty girl who hesitated to cross lest she wet her clothes. The older monk swept her up in his arms without pausing in his stride or his conversation, put her down at the other side and strode on.

The younger monk was spluttering with horror and indignation. 'A girl', he said, 'in your arms, and you a monk?' and he went on saying it. At last the older man came out of his thoughts and listened to the loud complaints. 'Oh,' he said, 'that girl? *I* put her down at the ford'.

Now laugh, not at the story for it needs no laughter, but at yourself, and everything. *At* yourself and *with* everything else. Did you realise that Zen Buddhism is the only school of training in the world which uses laughter, good fat belly laughter, as a sign of health and indeed a sign of attainment? Everywhere in the monasteries in which I stayed was the sound of laughter, that and the great bronze bell and the music of running water. So try to lighten your load; put a great laundry basket in the middle of the bedroom floor and throw something into it each morning when you rise. And instead of your breathing exercises yell with laughter. What will the neighbours think? That a neighbour has gone mad. They will be wrong. It will be a neighbour gone sane, and that much nearer to enlightenment.

Yours laughing as I drop it,

LETTER 45

Dear Sally,

You asked me after the talk last night on life in Zen monasteries about the use of ritual and how it fitted in with Zen. So did Mary, so you might show this reply to her. It puzzled me when I was in Japan. Here is the technique of direct action, more direct than any in the world, and yet, as the lecturer said, the monks get up in the middle of the night and have a service which includes pure ritual, and highly rehearsed and worked-out ritual at that. Nor can it be said that it is a sop for the public; there aren't any public there! I can see the answer, but it is not easy to describe. All creation is of two ingredients, life and form, the idea and its expression. While in the world of duality, therefore, to talk of anything direct is only an ideal, emphasis on the minimum of technique and periphrasis— (which means arguing 'about it and about' as in Omar's great quatrain.) We must use *some* means to the end, and Zen monks are allowed and indeed encouraged to study the few great scriptures used in Zen. They must also discipline their bodies, and they work in the fields or grounds or kitchen. They must also do something about the emotions and here they have great beauty everywhere, but save in writing or painting (for the few) very little means of artistic expression. Now ritual is very old, as old as man, and from the earliest times it has been used for magic, which is only the scientific use of natural forces not at that time known to science— (the telephone would have been magic in the days of Queen Elizabeth, and much of unorthodox healing is still magic today). Also, collective action is a valuable off-set to the individual work of each monk towards his own enlightenment. So, I think the habit grew up, and it would be interesting research to find out how and when and where. The effect, at any rate, is tremendous, as I saw it in the Jodo Sect as well as in Soto Zen. The physical control of immobility, the swift rhythmic movements, the fine chanting, the highly charged mental concentration making the room vibrate with power, all this at 4 a.m. with the first light of a winter's dawn stealing delicately through the pearl-grey paper screens that stood alone between us and the snow, all this I shall never forget. No self was there, but questing minds, the conscious units of All-Mind; it was a terrific experience.

Ritual has its uses all right, and if used as a *hoben*, as the Japanese call it, a means to an end, 'right'. But clung to, needed, it is a hindrance, and a barrier to the direct approach which leads, so they say, to Zen.

Permit me, Madam, to have the honour to remain, your ever humble and obedient servant—

and that is harmless ritual,

LETTER 46

Dear Mary,

So life is all too complicated? Complicated possibly and probably; too complicated, no. For it must be so. You know the Chinese saying—In the beginning a man sees mountains as mountains and trees as trees; then he grows a little and mountains are no more mountains and trees no longer trees. Then he attains enlightenment and mountains are once more mountains and trees are once more trees. The peasant and the child and the idiot have this in common, that they have simple minds, and simple lives. Then with the growing child, or a later life of the peasant and a better life of the idiot, simplicity fades and the complexity of right and wrong, good and bad, true and false emerges. We are all in that stage, and things must be very complicated indeed and very difficult before the very complexity drives us to seek the solution in the only field in which it can be found—Non-duality. As we approach we move again towards simplicity. As self is dropped its vast array of wants and hopes and fears and dislikes drop with it. We learn to want nothing, or much less, to 'feel' the right thing to do, to be unaffected by what does not belong in what Marcus Aurelius called the 'Ambit of our moral purpose'. The great man is very 'simple-minded'; so often is the great poet for the same reason, that his values are intuitive, and it is the mind, as you will know, that creates the complications. Walk on, towards simplicity.

Simply your friend,

LETTER 47

Notes from a Talk to the Zen Class

I said in Class at the beginning of this session that the Zen technique is not concerned with morality. This is strictly true, but it is a dangerous truth. And it is so potentially dangerous, because it is so easy to slide into the thought—if all is illusion, and nothing in a world of duality of any real importance, what does it matter what we do, with other people's money or wives or, for that matter, lives? This is what Dr Suzuki means when he talks of methods used to combat antinomianism, which I found to be a sixteenth century German sect that held that the Christian morality did not bind them. So bear this in mind in talking to your friends about their troubles, or your own, for I don't want you to hand on as my views what are only half of them.

I think, for example, that the 'three fires' of hatred, lust and illusion have immediate importance in the Zen life, and for this reason, that anything which is an action of the seeking mind which increases the sense of duality must be a further barrier to the experience of Non-Duality, which for most of us begins as a sense of oneness. The only criterion I know of value in active ethics is —Does the action contemplated (or more often, alas, done) tend

H   113

towards unity or diversity? Does it move towards the One or away from it? Does it heal, make whole, join and help, or does it injure, hurt and sunder? If the act is mere self-indulgence, as excessive smoking, or even drinking, it may be lamentable from several points of view but it does not immediately increase the sense of separation which is our basic illusion; the same may apply to fun and games on the sexual plane between those free to indulge. This is not 'right', in the sense that it is ideal or even the best we can do on the Way; but from the Zen point of view it is not actively harming another form of life. I would put spiteful gossip as a hundred times more harmful to the student of Zen than a party at which he got disgracefully tight. And failure to help another in distress, financial, emotional, or what you will, is a worse action than retaining the gentle illusion of the Virgin Mary as a Comforter to whom to pray in trouble. The test, then, is does the action separate, for to hurt another in any way *must* drive a further wedge in your mind between your self and his, or hers. We *are one*, that is the perpetual fact to remember. According as we live that truth we are moving to enlightenment.

LETTER 48

Dear Rodney,

Of course I will lend you Lily Abegg's *Mind of East Asia*, or any other book you want. You are now so much better balanced that I rejoice to find you a budding scholar. But don't get tied to books or you will get indigestion. The secret is to teach what you know, to hand on nearly as fast as you digest your reading. Why? For many reasons. First, wisdom is like blood, it lives while it flows. When it is sealed up it goes bad in the body in which it flowed. So with wisdom. We have no right to retain for ourselves what we find to be true. There is always, somewhere near you, someone who knows even less but desperately needs some crumb of comfort in the darkness of *avidya*. Look to your *Voice of the Silence*. 'Give light and comfort to the toiling pilgrim, and seek out him who knows still less than thou, who in his wretched desolation sits starving for the bread of Wisdom, without a teacher, hope or consolation, and let him hear the Law'. (I quote from memory but the sense is all right). And secondly, as fast as you empty your-

self of what you have learned the void will be filled. Give out and
you get, pass on and you will receive. That is good mechanics and
good sense. The wider the conduit pipe of the one life into you
the wider must be the outlet. Draw down, digest, pass on, with
your own added experience and in your own words. Thus the
Buddha, and I and you can do no less in purpose and attempt.

Good studying, and teaching,

LETTER 49

Dear Martha,

So you're losing your friends. Good riddance. I am sorry to be so
brutal but I mean it. What is a friend? Some one at or about your
level of attainment on the plane on which you are friend. Physical
friends as at golf, or dancing, which may not go deep. Emotional
friends, lovers may be, or just great affection, at any age or stage or
sex. Or mental mates, with the same ideals, ideas and way of approach to reality. (I leave out karmic friends from past lives, for
these do not leave you as such, though they may die or go away).

But we do not grow at the same rate, and we can grow out of our
friends as we grow out of our clothes. In which case let them go.
These friends of yours have let you go because, as you say, they
think you are becoming queer. So you are, to them, and they can
be very boring, if you face it, to you. So walk on, and make new
friends at your new level. Or is your real trouble a lack of courage
to go on living in a community which regards you as queer? Have
courage, moral courage which is so much nobler than mere physical
courage, which can be amazingly selfish. You will need great courage
of all kinds on the higher levels of the mountain, strength to face
doubt, temptation, exhaustion, lack of guts and drive. You may as
well begin to develop it now. Make books your friends, and the
Class when you can come, and then—your Self. It is the Universe
when you find it to be so, and you will never hereafter be alone.
As for Jim, he adores you. You have him as a friend, and a married
couple that are basically great friends have the best link in the
world for a happy marriage. And you have music, and the babies
(I nearly forgot them) and when all else utterly fails you, though
most respectfully,

ME.

LETTER 50

Notes from a Talk to the Zen Class

So many of you are now complaining of a sudden crop of troubles, physical, emotional and mental, that it is time I warned you that I expected such results and hoped for them. They are a sign of progress, the inevitable result of the new efforts made. It is an occult law as old as spiritual development that any real effort to advance internally, if I may use that phrase, will produce changes, uncomfortable if no worse, in all the departments of life, internal and external. Surely the reasons are obvious. You are suddenly, possibly when no longer young, diverting the current of life into new channels, with protest from the old ('I liked those violent sexy films') and from the new ('Ten minutes of that is enough—now I'll go back to my detective story'). Cutting new channels of thought, of relative values or habit of reaction, is very hard work, back-breaking spade work, and it needs to be done gently but unceasingly. It must be gently done because the law of action-re-action is inexorable; effort produces an exactly equal and opposite result. This effort is, as it were, a challenge to the Cosmic Accounts Department. The speed at which you are receiving the accumulated effects of past action is speeded up, and you are, as one expressed it, calling down your karma on your head. Look at it another way. There is always tension in the mind, and rightly so in a metaphysical sense, for we live in a field of the opposites, and in that bi-polar field all tension is life and the absence of it Nirvana or death. The new efforts, in a hitherto little used field, must change the tensions, increasing and diminishing each of the thousand pairs of them, and the resulting adjustment of the mind in all its departments itself involves new strain. The change of values can be as upsetting as the change in ideas, for what was of prime importance is seen as of no importance and the matter of sole importance is something entirely new. The new force, or new release of force into new channels, break down, sometimes violently, old forms of thought and belief and behaviour. Here, again, is a cause for strain and unsettlement, though always for the good. Finally, all this change affects one's attitude to environment, and thus, as you have been taught in the doctrine of Karma, the environment itself; and

as the circumstance change, so do you, the two being once more a
pair of opposites in the bi-polar field. How all these changes affect
you depends, of course, on you, and the index to your development
may be the way in which you can 'cope' with the changes. They
may be a mental malaise, with periods of depression, doubt, and
sudden joy; or of temper and peevishness, 'hurt feelings' and the
like, which surprise and embarrass you; or even of illness or un-
explainable accident. Or things go wrong in your environment,
people get ill, or you lose your job, or maid, or flat, or security.
But all this must be so, and you will now see why I am worried,
not by your worries, but at some dear soul who carries on placidly
with *nothing* happening, as I call happening, at all! I know well the
great herbalist, Mrs C. F. Leyel. When her patients complained
that after a few weeks of her herbal 'drops' the disease was worse,
she would greet them with 'excellent'; only when the symptoms
suddenly disappeared and health was restored did the patient
cease to complain. So it is with all healing, true medicine pushes
out the poisonous causes, from mind and emotions to the body,
and from organs, may be, to the skin. Often the last trace of the
trouble is a skin eruption and then, the illness is over. To attempt
to remove symptoms, as with drug therapy, is to defy nature, not
to assist her. I therefore rejoice when you get worse, for I know
you will then get better!

So accept your sufferings; you caused them and now, with your
efforts to achieve Non-action, you are having the self-expedited
effects. So I wish you fruitful suffering, and lots of it!

LETTER 51

Dear Billy,
This won't do at all. You heard what I said in Class last week
about increased troubles of all kinds. Now you tell me of yours and
complain that it isn't fair that after so much trouble at home you
should have the same with your boss and your job. Go for the
word 'fair'; what do you mean by it? It sounds as if you still had
the idea of Someone, some God, some Power Divine which is
punishing you for what you have done. Karma is a Law but there
is no Law-giver—do get that into your head. The laws of electricity
don't need God to run them, and the laws of thermodynamics

117

get on very nicely without the Buddha to intervene. None punishes or rewards you for what you do, nor even says thank you. It is you that produce the effects and suffer the consequences, though you affect all living things in the process. In brief, and you have heard me say this many times, we suffer *from* our sins, not *for* them. So stand up; don't lean on God or any other Extracosmic Force. Blame yourself for all you don't like about you, and take it on the chin. You will then be a man, and not a limpet, standing up and not leaning against a Guru or a bar, or any other extraneous piece of furniture.

Yours, but not to lean against,

LETTER 52

Dear Mrs Welling,

I note your complaints about the rheumatism, and I think you really do think it is all my fault. What have you done to deserve it? I know you write as if this were a joke, but is it wholly? All suffering is deserved, or the whole Universe is chaos and hell incarnate. Without Karma where is there sense in anything, but with it all is sanity and justice and harmony restored. You hope I pity you? That we deserve our suffering has no bearing on sympathy or pity. If a friend gets tight and drives into a lamp-post it is his fault in every sense that he suffers from multiple injuries. He deserved his suffering, and clearly so, but is that a reason for not feeling sorry for him? You must distinguish a profound understanding of the law of Karma from compassion for all forms of suffering in everybody, everywhere. The law is the exquisite balance of cause-effect. As we sow, so do we reap; we are what we have done. But it may be said that the more our suffering is knowingly deserved the more pity is needed, for to all else is added the agony, as it may be, of remorse. Or it might be said that the less we see that our suffering is deserved the more pity we deserve, for to the effects of our causation is added the thick veil of *avidya*, ignorance, from the blindness of which we shall probably do it again. So take your own suffering, add to it the equivalent of all the world, and know that all is the effect of past causes immutably worked out, without passion or mercy, variation or ill-will. Now add compassion for those who lie in jail as the sequence of their causing. They deserve what they have

118

got, may be, but need our sympathy to bear the consequences of their deserts. If a man is murdered in the prime of life you are apt to *think against* his murderer with horror, hate, self-righteous indignation, and much more. But *he* needs your help to bear the consequences, his deserts. He will suffer from his wrong-doing, *from* it not merely *for* it; but think of him as he waits for three hours, as one sat recently, while the jury decided the verdict whether he should live or die. He suffered hell, that man, and I for him while we waited for the verdict.

The pattern of life, then, is—suffering everywhere, everyday for everybody, from our own foolish acts; and sympathy for all who suffer, in which you need not utterly exclude yourself.

Good suffering, in which is blended all my sympathy at your deserts,

LETTER 53

Dear Bungy,

Talk to me of Jung, at any time and at any length, and correct my errors in attempting to apply his teaching, for he is one of the greatest minds alive and I think the greatest in the West. But do not talk to me of psychologists as a bunch save as we discuss the best mechanic to examine a car when it develops alarming noises under the bonnet. They are, I think, the only body of men and women on earth who have still the power to annoy me collectively. Even car-park attendants, civil servants and waitresses in tea-shops must be accepted as human, but psychologists? How *can* one react with cool serenity to the insufferably irritating delicate contempt which most psychologists quite unsuccessfully conceal at the mere mention of spiritual experience? 'Yes', they seem to say, with bright and brittle smile, 'the children are progressing nicely, and when finally released from the present phase of post-pubertal ego-determined affect-repressed hetero-compulsion (or bilge to that effect) will enter the tertiary level of comparative integration . . . ' Poor poops; they mean well but are actually proud of the concrete ceiling carefully built above their heads lest a breath of roses, the laughter of the dawn-wind as it chases dead leaves round the garden, the imprecations of the Greeks of old at the mangling of their lovely language into this polysyllabic obscenity should—where was I?—Oh yes, disturb their amiable and insufferably complacent smiles. Yes, they rile me at times. Jung and a very few others stand as the Great Hills of the Himalayas, their heads of awareness in the heights of Wisdom; the rest are mechanics, cleaning the petrol pipes and carburetters of the machine of the lower mind. Well, well, we must work with them, for what they are now discovering, even if it does not approach in some respects the knowledge of Buddhists as written down 2,000 years ago, is a great advance for the benefit of mankind. In any new or newly discovered science there will always be the underlings to degrade it—the same applies to Zen. But psychology is a coming science, and in one sense is the ultimate science, concerned as it is with the human mind, and we *must* work with it. Meanwhile, it sets that ceiling just where Zen technique is aimed at breaking through. Our task in the West is hard enough already, with such an absorption in the intellect as the Japanese never knew, and we need help from psychology, not a hindrance. When they arrive at Karma and Rebirth there will be a sudden break; after that we shall have them chattering of All-Mind.

Now snap out of that dull machinery of thought, whether normal, abnormal, schizoid or plain nuts, and go for THAT which laughing awaits you, ever-glorious beyond the latest science and the utmost —ology.

Your friend till forced to undergo treatment,

and then no longer,

LETTER 54

Dear Bungy,

So you wish to bite me for my 'outburst' on psychologists in the West. Excellent. Now we can talk. How do we fight? Matching an incipient schizoid tendency with an ambivalent social reaction indicating pre-pubital psychopathy? But let's be serious. Of course there are very fine men and women in this pioneer field, which, as I said last time, must be the final science. And I agree that every specialised field must, as it were, delimit itself in advance, or it would not be specialisation. But there is a difference. The mystic can say 'I am not a philosopher,' the astronomer 'I am not a physiologist' (though these distinctions are rapidly beginning to 'blend and blur', as Rupert Brooke said of the centuries at Grantchester). And psychology is concerned, I presume, with the structure and functioning of the psyche or mind. Within these limits all is to the practitioner in a subjective field. What matters to him is what the pupil or patient feels and believes, its objective truth being almost irrelevant. Thus, as Jung says somewhere, God may or may not exist in the field of metaphysics but in the mind He may be, as a force, a powerful reality. So far, so good, but so many psychologists fail to adopt a modest and right attitude to workers outside their field, that of a respectful, tolerant friendliness. I remember Miss Horner, the great Pali specialist, going through the MS of my Pelican *Buddhism*. All to do with Pali she criticised and if need be corrected, firmly and even dogmatically. That was right, she was the expert and I the child. But anything outside that she would not touch. It might or might not be correct, she did not know. But she did not sneer, covertly or otherwise, at statements concerning aspects of Buddhism not in her specialist field. The psychiatrist, who is the psychologist in action, too often adopts the patronising attitude of a headmaster with an over-imaginative child, and does not conceal his view that many of these beliefs and theories are only foolish imagination, and that those who practise them, not excepting Jung himself, are straying from the path of sanity. That this my view is right is surely fortified by their description of the ideal man, the end-product, as it were, of all therapy. From a nasty mess to 'integration', from integration to 'individuation', such is the ladder (at the moment), but what a dreary creature is the individuated man! From the Buddhist point of view, the Path begins with such and the end, even a single flash of Zen satori, is aeons ahead of the nicely tidied up and sorted out and balanced mind which they hope to re-create and then eject from the consulting room as 'finished'. It is like the mechanic in the garage who says after weeks of work, 'There you are, Sir, that's the best I can do.' It may be, but the result is nevertheless an ancient Austin 7 and that much short of the supreme product of Messrs Rolls and Royce.

Nevertheless I repeat my firm belief that we *must* work in with psychologists and not quarrel with them, for this is the field in which Buddhism could be of most immediate service to the West; the latest findings of the greatest of psychologists, led by Jung, can bridge the gap as nought else between the minds of East and West.

And now I wait for the observation of the first psychologist, or 'trick-cyclist', to whom you show this letter. 'Tut tut. The child is peevish—a clear case of . . . ' It may be—what excellent material for my self-control!

Yours probably psychopathically,

LETTER 55

Dear Caplan,

I quite see your difficulty, and others have told me the same. But in a group of thirty people the intellectual level cannot be the same, nor does there exist any 'average'. It is true that most of the greatest mystics, as well as the greatest philosophers, have been highly intellectual people, however humble their birth, and the Zen Masters of old had obviously first class minds. By this standard it would be useless to have anyone in the Class who had not a well-developed and trained intellect, or at least the equivalent in the field of the emotions. But we have to begin somewhere, and the first necessity is to *want* enlightenment, and to want it very badly indeed. I therefore take the view that anyone showing genuine *want* is worth considering, and if the want is not too selfish, and the difficulties are fairly faced, let him or her begin. As to growth or development this takes place on several planes simultaneously, and possibly quite out of proportion to each other. Some people become for the first time emotionally balanced; others develop as never before the capacity of clear thought; others just feel more integrated, in the sense that all of them seems to function more as a whole. But behind this, possibly leaving the man we know almost unaffected, there can be and I believe very often is, a spiritual growth which the brain may not know. I humbly believe that I recognize this intuitively as time goes on, though I could not explain just what that growth consists of or whence it comes. (It comes of course from the deeps within, but you know what I mean).

So don't worry about not being on the intellectual plane of some of the others. Believe me, some of them are the worst bound in the field of duality by that very intellect, and are not, from the spiritual point of view, to be envied at all. Walk on, for you are cooking nicely, though the process may be at times uncomfortable!

LETTER 56

Dear Rodney,

All that happens happens right! Put that into your pipe and smoke it, for it is absolutely, in the true sense of that term, true. This applies to timing. There is a right and wrong time for everything, as a right and wrong place, means, motive and intent. You can't get to satori by any particular time for it is beyond time, and just when you will have an experience, great or small, in this life or in the next, depends on many factors, most of which are for the moment outside your control. Nor will intensity of effort alone suffice; the very effort, as I thought I had explained sufficiently, can, and often does produce the counter-force which will stultify the effort. Zen lies on an exquisitely balanced and inconceivably narrow middle way, with right effort and no-effort as a pair of the opposites.

True acceptance and sulky indifference, however, are not a pair of opposites but the right and wrong variety of the same thing. To accept is a mighty spiritual virtue, and a fairly rare one. It is far more than thinking—'Well, let him go to hell in his own way', or, 'I suppose I *must* buy a new carpet sweeper though it is very expensive', or 'I accept the fact that we have to move but . . .' *There are no 'buts' in acceptance.* There will be no Zen so long as the facts of circumstance have any felt relation with oneself. To accept in that mood is not to accept, but to resent, to agree with a scowl. There are still two separate things, your self and the event; Zen is not two things, or one thing, it is Zen—and no self. Until you can accept everything so heartily and completely that you and it are one you are fighting Zen, not seeking it. This does not mean a spineless lying down under oppression or injustice, though it is often the best course for you—if you wish to drop self—to pursue. And it *never* means that you lie down while a friend is unjustly attacked, or in need of assistance against the local Borough Council, or the like. Your job is to do the job in hand, cheerfully, immediately, happily, not *because* of *anything*, or with any motive or thought of result, but because it *is* the next job to be done. Say to yourself in every situation, pleasant or unpleasant, easy or plum impossible—'Zen is One and not two'. Abstract your self from it as the cause and creator of all the trouble, and drop it in the dust-bin (all right, trash-can if you must be American) and leave it there! You have to have your teeth out? Very well, you have to have your teeth out. It will hurt, and be expensive, and embarrassing at the office. Very well, it will be. Now what? Grumbles, fear, complaint, annoyance—ad lib? If you wish. But you will still have your teeth out and it will still hurt and be expensive and embarrassing at the office. Now remove yourself from the whole horrible business. The next job to be done—to ring up the dentist. Very well, ring up!

Yours brutally,

LETTER 57

Dear Mary,

I know well what you mean when you say you feel like a hermit crab without a shell, naked in a crowd with sticks and stones, defenceless and correspondingly cross and fearful. This is a phase of progress and indicates that you are truly 'walking on'. We live our lives behind self-erected barricades of make-believe, behind the mask of a personality which is how we shouldlike to appear, but quite untrue. The strain gets terrible, and the Self within longs to be strong enough to drop it suddenly and be less splendid but more free, smaller perhaps in the eyes of men but true, instead of an exhausting, living lie. So drop your defences, or let your progress within have that result, and *don't pick them up again*. Watch the process of re-assuming this armour of falsehood and stop it. 'This above all, to thine own self be true' is magnificent advice but the self of thyself is the Self, the inner man, not the boss in the office. And, the rest of the quotation is worth remembering. 'And it must follow as the night the day, thou canst not then be false to any man.' Meanwhile we *are* false, to most men (though husbands and wives, it is said, know all). What are one's friends but those with whom we may be natural, peevish at times, depressed and fearful? We need their service in this way. Why? Because we must have times when the defences are lowered and we can be what we are, at our worst maybe, but such as we are. But the fact that we *must* at times lower the fences shows that for most of the time we have them. Why? Because we lack the courage to be natural, and fear the ridicule of those about us were they to see us as our pitiful, naked

selves. Yet it is true that our friends probably love us for the compli-
ment we pay them of taking off our armour, and leaving it in the hall
with our coats and hats and other anti-weather devices. Drop your
defences, then, be frightened but be naked. So we shall love you the
more and you be the happier, the stronger, and free.

This reminds me, (for I have a most disobedient mind that
scampers off after every lady friend of thought-association) of what
one of you said in class about anger and hate arising. I have re-
membered it and applied it often. It is the speed with which we
cope with the thought or emotion *as it arises* that may decide whether
we successfully cope with it or not. Take anger, for example. At
something someone does or says we begin to feel angry. Constant
exercise in being 'mindful and self-possessed' will produce the
power to react *at once* to the invader, to hit him at once and hit him
hard, or, if you prefer it, to drop the thought before it can be given
the strength to grow. As one of you wrote to me, 'Do not attempt
to root out hatred, fear, anxiety. Impossible! But pay attention
to them, not to the outward events which have called up these
emotions—they are no longer present—but to the emotions themselves.' This is grand advice, and true training. The event was
neither good nor bad save as you labelled it, but your reaction
should have been in your power to decide or at least control. Forget
the external fact and look to the internal reaction; that is your
concern always. And when you once perceive the anger for what
it is, with a mind serene, 'untouched by circumstance', you can
readily let it drop. 'What, you again? I thought I told you not to
come to the house again'—as to a dirty old tramp, (or perhaps
that applies more to dirty old thoughts, but the principle is the
same).

And while I am about it I might as well leap to another thought,
the necessity of keeping the 'higher mind' (I know no better term)
free from interference from lower interruptions and influences.
The Master K. H. gave the reasons when advising A. P. Sinnett
about the writing of his book *Esoteric Buddhism*. 'It is upon the
serene and placid surface of the unruffled mind that the visions
gathered from the invisible find a representation in the visible
world. Otherwise you would vainly seek those visions, those flashes
of sudden light which have already helped to solve so many of the

minor problems and which alone can bring the truth before the eye of the soul.'

> But I am chattering,
> Good night.

Dear Martha,

What's gone wrong? You seemed so settled in your life, so busy working along Zen lines within the framework of your home, that I am puzzled to see this entirely new factor of—is it fear—appearing in your talk to me? I did not mention it in our interview as I was not certain I was right. It seems that you expect peace where you can never find it, and are shying at the idea of the prolonged and bitter war which *must* be fought, and to victory, before the self is ended and the goal in sight. Let's face it, peace is a dream and an idle dream until the war within is over, one way or the other, and to lose it is irrevocable death. So face that this fight, the warfare of self versus Self, the demands of the part or the high destiny of the whole, the flames of lust and hate and illusion or the serenity of inward sight, is a fight that has been declared. You may win or lose but you cannot sit on the edge as at a football match and cheer the winner. *You* are the winner and loser, but which 'you' wins and which loses? That is for you and for you alone to say. So long as within each mind there is war to the end between self-ishness or self-lessness there cannot be peace or comfort in that mind. In the same way, when men get together in groups and each want this and that for their side there will be warfare, even though the group be as large as a nation and the warfare is global. That is why I say that to talk of peace at a conference table is a waste of words; until the parties *want* peace there will not be peace but war. When they *want* peace it is easy enough to 'make' it. But so long as the individual is torn within by his own private war, how can he be a peace-maker at the conference table? So war there will be until the last human being has won that war within. As I said, (and I thought it a jolly good phrase to come impromptu when talking to ten thousand people on the Ramlila Ground at Delhi) 'the price of peace is self'. So get up and fight, not your neighbour but yourself, for your neighbour, whether he knows it or not, has his hands full

with his own battle. Fight the greed and lust and hate and spiteful-
ness in your own mind. And the illusion which breeds your wrong
ideas, of which the last is belief in twoness. True, you do not show
these horrid facets of the mind, nor do I—many of them—but I
know that I have them and I expect you have them too. So get up
and fight, wholeheartedly, with the moral courage of a martyr
and the yells of laughter of a Zen practitioner. Throw fear away
and *bite* the enemy. Fear nothing, for it is only self that fears and
you are fast destroying this stronghold of your fear. If there is
nothing that fears there will be no fear. Kill the fearer and let joy
be unconfined! Up Guards and bite 'em, as the Duke of Wellington
might have said. Are you laughing, at me, or at you, or everything?
That's better.

Yours in the front line,

LETTER 59

Dear Brampton,
I know it is difficult at your age to be free of the fetters of a life's
hard thinking. But use the machinery of thought as you know it
to come with me beyond it. The Western line of intellectual
approach to any problem or facet of truth is a straight one. 'This
being so, that follows.' 'That being so it is safe to infer this.'
And so on. In the end there is a direct onslaught on the subject/
object, or so it seems. But is it? The intellect (we have been over this
before) uses words with which to build concepts, both being
symbols of and therefore substitutes for direct experience of that
truth. The truth invested, so to speak, is ringed about with concepts until a new one appears, being a building composed of the
old ones, and the discovery is given a new label as a new truth.
So it may be in one sense, but it is a cage in which a fragment of the
truth is caught, as Pierrot tried to catch the butterfly of his beloved
in his hat in the ballet Carnaval. It is not truth but the clothes of
truth which are now so proudly displayed at the next Annual
Conference of that learned Society.

Now consider the Eastern approach, so well described in Lily
Abegg's *Mind of East Asia*. The Eastern approach is not direct but
devious, (note the paradox, that this is 'direct' action). A little logic
here, a little emotion there, a hint of art, a joke, a paradox and

silence. This complex, devious, infinitely subtle approach leaves room for the total mind's absorption of the new idea. It is applied as understood, felt as thought, and known by a flash of the intuition that all the logic in the world will never achieve. This makes possible the Zen logic of no-logic about which Dr Suzuki speaks so deliciously and writes again and again. A is A, say the logicians. Therefore A is not at the same time not-A. A is A, say the gentlemen of Zen; *therefore* A is also and at the same time not-A. 'How?' yell the Western intellectuals, as well as the ordinary man in the street, who regrets to point out that the man of Zen is talking through his hat. The man of Zen takes the logician by the hand and leads him back to the 'moment' (beyond time) when there was neither A nor not-A, when both were unborn facets of one primordial Reality. In THAT, as the Indian philosophers call it for want of a better name, is A *and* not-A, both true/untrue and neither True. After all, I have brought you to agree that every single statement made is untrue, in that it is at the best partial. And no part is true or can be, only the whole, and the whole includes the opposite of the statement made. Very well, A is A—that is true. A is not A. *That* is true. Which is truer? Neither, save relatively. Bump! did you hear the bump? That was Reality falling down into relativity. Relatively, of course, A is A and A is not-A or B. But absolutely *both* are true. Now you see the limitations of the intellectual approach. It may achieve relatively true results. It can never achieve absolutely true results; the East can and does—but not with the intellect!

Yours as ever,

LETTER 60

Dear Mr Wilmington,

Who said Zen demanded that we sell all we have and give it to the poor? It is the first I have heard of it! In the first place Zen is not concerned with outer behaviour, with the wealth or poverty of the personality, and secondly, if the person concerned is in lawful possession, as you are, of a host of lovely things, it is the hand of karma that gave it him, and with it the responsibility to see that so much beauty is rightly used. Surely it is clear from all Zen writing that the alleged Theravada teaching of running away from life (which I do not believe to be the true teaching of the Theravada

128

school), is anti-Zen, if such be possible. There is nothing to run away from and no one to run away. The man and his circumstances are from the Zen point of view one and the same thing, or two things related as the two sides of a coin. You cannot successfully run away from riches any more than you can run away from poverty, and the attempt in both cases must fail. What matters is not what you possess, of health, or wealth or honour or glory, but what you do about it, how you use it, how you react to it. In other words, to what extent, if at all, you are *attached to it*. Where there is non-attachment how shall it hurt a man though he own the earth? Where there is attachment, even of the very poor man to his favourite teapot, there is attachment; the mind is not free. In this way you can see how life, with its pleasures and horrors, its wealth and poverty, is the field in which we fight self to a finish, the gymnasium, as I unctuously wrote in youth, in which we develop the muscles of the soul (I did really!) It matters not, therefore, in what circumstances we live, of health or illness, comfort or none, in this house or job or town or in some other; what matters is what we *do* with the surroundings of the personality, knowing that the mind within, the higher Self, or call it what you will, is, or should be, learning to be 'the mind that alights nowhere', which nothing on earth or in heaven can bind or even assoil. Here, in this life, shall we attain Enlightenment, or not at all. Here 'in this body six feet in length', as the Buddha says in the Pali Scriptures, 'is the world, and the origin of the world, and the ceasing of the world, and likewise the Way that leadeth to the ceasing thereof'. Here, not somewhere else, in a monastery, or in heaven. So keep your treasures while you want them, for while you want them you can never get rid of them, even if you give them away! How much better to use them wisely, give some to those who have none and will love them, make all available from time to time to a wider circle, and leave them to those who will love them as you once did. It is a responsibility you have, not a houseful of rubbish to throw away.

But don't confuse attachment and indifference. You can and should cultivate non-attachment, but that is a delicately balanced middle way between attachment and repulsion, wanting and not wanting, desiring and hating. You can do many things with money but to be indifferent to it leads you nowhere at all. Indifference is negative, therefore partial, and to the extent that it is positive equally betrays a distinction in the mind which, like all others, is 'falsely imagined'.

So love your treasures, for their beauty, their craftsmanship, their symbolism of Reality—then let them go. Thus you will not be bound by them, nor they to you. Each will be free and both contented. Do I personify them? I do. As Li-Po said of the mountain about which he wrote so many and such lovely poems—'We never get tired of each other, the mountain and I.'

Be poor then, as one who lays up no treasure on earth, but don't lay it up in heaven either. Use it, love it and let it go!

Sincerely,

LETTER 61

Notes from a Talk to the Zen Class

For what I have to say this evening I want you to accept one matter of doctrine as a reasonable and working hypothesis, and it is this. There are in us at least two 'selves', which for want of a better term I will call the higher and the lower. The lower, the personality, is far stronger and more established than we like to think, yet, although it is, as the world implies, no more than a mask through which the actor speaks, it is often taken for the actor and in extreme cases *becomes* the actor. But it is an illusion, and so long as we allow it to have separate life it is a serious hindrance on the way. You think of yourself as of this sex, age, appearance, class, race, type and so on. You are not. These are the clothes which the Self, the truer, higher though still impermanent and changing Self wears at the moment. When I speak to you, therefore, individually, I have to ignore all that I see, and all the tricks of the personality, endearing or the reverse, which may blind my eyes to the man or woman within, the 'pilgrim soul' of Western poetry. But I have a further difficulty. I have to lay down my own personality to look at you; otherwise I am blinded by a vast edifice of my own, compounded of age, sex, class, religious and educational background, race prejudice, philosophic and religious training, and so on. If, therefore, I am to communicate with you I must drop my self in order to penetrate, with the eye of the intuition, yours. I want you,

therefore, over Easter to set in motion a new habit of mind, to begin
to see with *your* true Self and to see the Self of your friends—and
your enemies. You will get shocks. You may find that those whom
you like you like for trivialities and that in fact you have little in
common. You will find that those you dislike you dislike for details
so unimportant that you will blush at the discovery. Undress yourself, rise up and look again with the eyes of Self, 'the pilgrim of
eternity', moving from life to life, shedding self, expanding the
higher mind and the intuition, learning, suffering, walking on.
What does *this* Self care if the woman next door has a raucous
voice, or the man you sit next to at the office teases you about your
hair? It is often as trivial as that. And you? Are *you* loved and
unloved for the qualities of Self or the trivia of your changing
personality? You would like to know! So try the double process,
of lifting above the self to see clearly, and stripping those about you
of their personalities, to look at them, may be, for the first time.

The importance of all this from the Zen point of view is surely
obvious. When a pupil enters the Master's room for San-Zen,
does the master care that he has an ugly face, or common voice,
or is extremely beautiful or very rich? These are the effects of
karma, to be accepted as 'pleasant or unpleasant', and of no spiritual
importance at all. He uses his 'inner eye' to see what is really
happening behind the mask of the man's personality. In the same
way the pupil tries to lift himself to the level of the Master's mind
and to receive help at that level. Their respective personalities
are, for that interview, not merely irrelevant but a nuisance, as each
must lay his own aside to get on with the job. This does not mean
that the Master is always 'cold' and impersonal, as you know well
from the visits we have received from such. The man who a moment
before was flashing lightning at the thought-bound pupil's darkened
mind may now receive with gratitude a cup of his special tea, or,
as I remember, an American cigar, and enjoy it thoroughly. Then
we can again play the fool (so good for us) and utterly enjoy the
humblest things, through our re-assumed personalities, but feeling
now as a man who, working in the snow, must wear warm clothes
which yet impede his movements. Later, as the outer self is purged
and reduced in power it will more and more reflect the real man,
or the *more* true man, and allow the tremendous spiritual strength
of the inner man to radiate, through the eyes and from the whole

of him, to make a pool of light about him in his humblest affairs.

But I want you to apply these truths more practically still, to the rest of you in the group. There is too much gossip still, not mere chatter about each other but actively unkind thoughts, which find expression in words and in deeds, done or not done. I know the spiritual effort you are making is apt to set one's nerves on edge, and people become more sensitive. But watch it. That may be a reason, but it is no excuse for unkind and even spiteful gossip. Use the new power, lift to your higher level, and look at this woman who so annoys you, this man whose habit of drawing attention to himself so sets your teeth on edge, and realize that this is all illusion, it just doesn't exist, and to the extent that it does seem real, refuse to let it affect you even at personality level. It will not hurt you any more than a single midge-bite will send you raving mad.

And now for the spiritual value of the habit. Why does Self seek Self, and in that communion find no differing? Because that Self is also the other man s Self, *all* other Selves, as sparks of one Flame, inseverable aspects of one Whole. Face to face two Selves shall find no severance; they are, and know that they are, one. But no two personalities shall know this secret, save through a glass, darkly. Here is true communion of love looking downwards called compassion, across, called friendship, or up, called devotion to the Beloved. These are based on the Prajna plane of the highest Self we can reach; the rest is the quarrelling and mating and fighting of animals, natural on *their* plane but no longer natural or right in our climb to the Goal.

So let us meet anew, leaving our personalities outside as we leave our coats; so shall we draw closer to one another, and to the realm of Non-duality.

LETTER 62

Dear Mary,

So you are tired of Zen? That you are tired I know, and generally 'fed up with everything'. Before you have the holiday you need, however, I shall brutally drive you to confess what bosh you are talking. First, *who* is tired? Your body, nerves, fretted emotions, worried lower mind—granted. These, as you well know, are *not* you, so you are *not* tired. What then? Tired of what? Of Zen?

Certainly not, for Zen is the force of life itself, of unlimited strength and joy and laughter; you mean, and don't snarl at me like that, that the self is weary of the effort of committing suicide. I am not surprised. Nearly all the bits of us kick fiercely at being firmly held under the guillotine, certainly the peevish, grabbing, spiteful self-ish little horror which yaps all the time to be noticed and petted and allowed its grubby little way. So let it off the lead just occasionally, but so that it does no harm. Stop your study and meditation for a week over Easter, for one can get stale in any form of training, but remember that the longer you stop the harder work it is to catch up again when you begin. (I find that a most annoying fact).

But to keep the engine warm, so to speak, just keep some phrase at the back of the mind, and let it pop up now and again and talk to you. May I suggest 'The hill goes up and down'?

> Yours in fun and games, and in the
> payment therefor,

LETTER 63

Dear Rodney,

Congratulations on the degree. Now, as you say, you will be very busy, but don't talk nonsense about therefore having 'little time for Zen'. I repeat, as I must have told a score of you, that you will have, then as now, *all* time for Zen, and indeed should order your life that you will have time for nothing else. Zen is not a matter of study, *or* meditation, *or* noble thinking *or* paradoxical super-sense. It is a new way of looking at things, of doing things, of seeing things as they are; a new technique for facing circumstances, for coping with problems, for living life. If you are not doing your 'Zen chores', as you call them, when sharpening a pencil, addressing a golf-ball, seeing a patient or washing your teeth, I repeat you will not find Zen when locked in a bedroom facing the wall. Do your study and meditation and deep thinking when you have time—and you will find you *have* time if you organise your day properly—but then do it *all the time*. You have to be in *some* focus of attention, balance of directed will-power, point of view, when doing all the things I said. Now develop the habit of deciding in advance what that attitude shall be. Make it the constant approach to reality which is also Reality—for all you do, feel, say and want to do. That is the Zen

life. The man of Zen is direct, fearless, certain and serene in *all* he is
and does. Get on with that!

Yours, direct at any rate in this,

LETTER 64

Dear Mary,

So now you are feeling hurt. From what you say you have every
right to be hurt if there is such a thing as being hurt being ever
right. But it isn't. *What* is hurt? Your self, in its emotional untidi-
ness, with horrid bits of egotism trailing round it like seaweed so
that the first person to come along and tread on a bit of it hurts
you? Well, cut off the seaweed! You say I don't understand. The
trouble is that I do, having tried to cope with at least 1,000 bits of
seaweed in my time. But the fact that the person hurt cannot be
reasoned with to see the folly of the hurtness is evidence that the
very experience of being hurt is irrational, because pertaining to the
subconscious of the patient. When it is merely pride or ambition that
is injured one can reason, and point out the experience to be merely
what it is. But when there is a puffed-up ego which has become so
identified with the individual that he or she does not even realise
that it is but an outer balloon of untrue ballyhoo, then the patient
cannot be made to see, at least at the time, what is happening.
I long to be allowed to use the brutal methods in these cases that
I have succeeded for years in using on myself. When I feel hurt
I pounce on the cause without delay and blast myself for the fatuous
folly of it, sneer at myself for a pride I should not have, for private
ambitions I should have dropped years ago, and kick myself on the
emotional ankles. With others I should love to be able to use the
Zen technique of curing anything off centre by driving it further
off-centre. When complaining of the heat, turn the fire on; of cold,
go and lie naked in the snow. So with emotions; I should love, when
a woman complains of being hurt, to hurt her far more badly,
to insult her, blast her until, at the end of a flood of tears she
suddenly worked through the fog of feeling to the sweet sunlight
of the inner Self's own vision of Reality. But I should need time
and a padded room for that, or the Lord Buddha knows what I
should be thought to be doing with the woman concerned!

So now snap out of it. Kick the furniture by all means; sulk, scream and burst into tears as needed; then put on your best hat and go shopping. And when convenient write to me and tell me all about it, burning the letter before posting, however, lest the postal authorities complain of the heat of it.

Once, when very small, I was taken to a new Church one Sunday afternoon, where my temporary 'aunt' told me the Church was God's House. At tea I was asked how I liked the service. I said, 'It was God's house, but I looked all round and he was out.' What brilliant precocity in terms of the Zen doctrine of the Void!

Now put that hat on.

With love always,

LETTER 65

Dear Sally,

So you're another getting tired, are you? Who is tired? Tired of what? You don't know? All right. Try the opposite and so restore the balance. All effort produces resistance, like pushing a pendulum, and even the best effort should be balanced with intelligent rest at times. But there can be awfully wrong effort, wrong because it is carefully done in the illusion that it is right. Beware of the illusion that something has been done which has only been half-done. It is not too difficult at our stage of development to act without thought of self, in the sense of unselfishly and spontaneously. But how much of it is spoilt by self-satisfaction at such nobly selfless acts? We must, as the masters say, not only throw away the thought of I but also the thought of No-I!

Meanwhile we live in tension, and rightly so in the world of duality. For the field of manifestation, of the Universe as of the littlest thought, is bi-polar, and all art, as you know it, and the art of life, is set out in that field. There is balance in the tension, for a magnet has two poles, and the stress and strain inherent in occasional imbalance is clear to all of us. So after much effort let there be some rest, but let the rest be intelligent and itself under control. I have said a thousand times that 'doing nothing' is rightly a part of our total life, but let the nothing be under control. Plan, that for a half hour or whatever it may be, or just five minutes or even a full day in bed, you will turn off all taps, of action, emotional meandering and deliberate thought, and *do nothing*. Don't think, worry, plan

135

or want; don't wonder, regret, hope or fear. *Do nothing*. Many a businessman today in the West has ten minutes flat on his back in the office after lunch, with the door locked; then he rises and feels a different man. But if you just want relaxation, decide what you will do and do that only. If you listen to fine music, *listen*; if you play patience, play carefully and well. If you read a detective story, read it and try to solve it. If in the garden, weed, and don't be planning a letter to the local Council about the behaviour of the woman next door. And so on. This is I believe right action. Then get up and do other right action, but equally and always under control. As for you, get down to the river and muck about with that boat. One day it might be persuaded to hold water . . .

LETTER 66

Notes from a Talk to the Zen Class

Sooner or later on the Way each man must turn and face his 'shadow'. Thus modern psychology, but the necessity for this experience, however named, is as old as occult training. The shadow is the self, the lower, animal, selfish and unworthy side of us, the self we despise in ourselves and would feign hide from our friends. But it is ours, we are it; it is as much part of the total man who climbs to enlightenment as the very will to climb. And as we must climb total, whole, entire or not at all, so we must first withdraw those portions of the total self which, from cowardice, self-lying or sheer ignorance, we have projected onto people, gods and things that stand, as does all 'circumstance', about us. The practice of withdrawal of projections can only begin when we realise how much of ourselves is projected, and for this some little study of psychology is wise. But we project whenever we blame another for what is the result of our own action. The doctrine of Karma should help the Buddhist to withdraw his projections, for better than most he has the means to appreciate that all his circumstance is self-begotten, and that there is no one to be blamed save himself for all that happens to him. We blame the Government always, and beyond it that shadowy God created by the folly of man called, nowadays, the State. In even greater unreason we put the blame on 'they' ('they don't give you a chance nowadays'). And in shorter focus we blame the boss, the weather, our rheumatism, failing sight and the Communists. We also blame atom bombs, our neighbours, that 'perfectly useless doctor' and the younger generation. To begin to withdraw all this is a tremendous undertaking. It needs, as Jung points out in a famous passage in his *Psychology and Religion*, a brave man. Yet he who succeeds in doing it even a little lifts thereby some portion of the world's great burden, reduces, in the words of *The Voice of the Silence* by just so much 'that mighty sea of sorrow formed of the tears of men'. It is wise indeed to argue with oneself in every unpleasant situation. What have I done to make it so; what can I do to change it, if need be changing something in myself? This slow and deliberate movement backwards, so to speak, into the deeps of the Self within, is the beginning of the journey home. In terms of Zen it is finding one's original face. It involves a total and willing acceptance of the worst of us as well as the best, of the dirty, mean and spiteful mind, the hate, the lying and the lust; it means that in thought at least we are willing to lie in the gutter with the drunk, the brutal thief, the prostitute, *as one of them*. And in terms of group activity it involves identification with the worst as well as the best of one's fellow students, with the irritating ways and manners of most of them as well as with the spiritual progress of the few. As the Master K. H. said in writing to A. P. Sinnett about the founding of the London Lodge, 'It is true manhood when one boldly accepts one's share of the collective Karma of the group one works with, and does not permit oneself to be embittered and to see others in blacker colours than reality, or to throw all blame upon one "black sheep", a victim specially selected.'

But to withdraw projections one must cease to lean. The student who is all set for Zen-experience must make that final burst alone. He will stand or run—and jump—with his own two feet beneath him, leaning and relying on nothing else, or God or man or doctrine, to support him in that hour. How many of us stand alone, or would be the same without teacher, scriptures, Society, group or dearest friend? And how many, thus alone, would be the same when stripped of reputation, honour, all possessions and the last vestige of good name? Yet thus shall we climb or not at all, totally, utterly, with grubby thought and selfish yearning; thus shall we reach the Gateless Gate where stands our Zen St Peter, and all of us or none pass through! Meanwhile, when your foot caught the chair

leg this morning, or you cursed when the vase was upset, were you
blaming . . . you?

Yours, whose answer would be
'probably not',

LETTER 67

Dear Bungy,

When I say 'Walk on', echoing the mighty Master of old, I mean,
for thus I understand that teaching, that we should walk on. I know
of no exception. Certainly it may be applied to the faint-hearted,
to those who halt by the wayside for want of enough Zen-breath.
But it also applies to you—who have sat, with a smile of revolting
unctuousness, on the comfortable seat of 'achievement' in order
to admire the view, and, what is far more horrible, to look with vast
compassion on the toiling multitude who are yet a number of
zig-zags of the mountain path below. We talked not long ago about
self-appraisal. This is not, you will admit, co-terminous with self-
praise. Contentment, satisfaction—hurl them away, arise and walk
on! Through fog and sunshine, hope and lamentation and despair,
in a hell of depression—you have not known that yet—in doubt,
that tears the bowels of the mind asunder or, in this at least more
worthy, in that incurable unrest of heart that comes with the first
and awful glimpse of the suffering of all mankind. Don't sit, and
don't be satisfied. Keep moving, fast or slowly, but always, always,
walking on! Do I speak with authority? I do, for I think that this
is my only virtue—that I do not stop.

Yours, a little breathless at times,

LETTER 68

Dear Silver,

So at last you have learnt to 'see straight'. Presumptuous man!
If only we could do that we should be there. For this is the doctrine
of Tathata, of seeing the 'suchness' of things, of seeing all things
as they are. Could we see one thing as it really is presumably we
could see all things as they really are, and thus perceive 'our original
face', and hear the voice of the Silence. But the eyes with which
we see thusly are not personal eyes; they are cosmic or rather pre-

cosmic eyes, before the illusion of duality was born. But we do see more and more straight as we patiently tear at our carefully woven veils of illusion. And this vision is, as you say, tremendously exciting. I have been re-reading for the umpteenth time the Mahatma Letters, and found a quotation by the Master K. H. from Tyndall, whoever he was. 'Facts looked at directly are vital; when they pass into words half the sap is taken out of them.' I like that. How lovely are the words of those who can see directly; how simple, certain and direct! But we shall learn the trick of it one day.

Sincerely,

LETTER 69

Dear Martha,

As an exercise in 'at least approaching vaguely in the direction of non-duality' may I recommend the following exercise. Take light and darkness, or silence and enormous sound. Or terrific effort and complete relaxation. Get each alternately clear in your imagining, than bang their heads together suddenly. Silly? I agree but it has worked with me before now, and I can get silence/sound fairly easily. Not a compromise but the sensation of both to the nth degree at the same time. The effort/rest is the most valuable. We all alternate between effort and rest, but if we can learn to use maximum effort while still in repose we are truly improving our selves as a machine for getting things done. In meditation the mind should be lifted as high as possible (effort) and poised in complete relaxation to receive it. Do this, one after the other, and then get the effort/repose position. Then hold it. Thus do I meditate, for in it there is no room for me, or for that matter for any such nonsense as meditation! Coo!

Yours as ever,

LETTER 70

Dear Crashaw,

You honour me by asking my advice in your difficult situation, but I shall honour you by refusing to advise you. It is, as you know, your own responsibility, and if I strongly advised you to say yes or no I should rob you of the merit of a right decision, and weaken your power to choose wisely next time. Part of my job in class is to help you people to stand on your own feet in all things, to lean on nothing and no one, not even on a teacher of my standard. Choose as you think right, letting the intuition speak if possible; then act and accept the consequences. To use first principles, do what you think right—then you will have done all you can. The consequences will be what they will be, and are not your concern.

But I can help to this extent, by offering what I believe to be the right principles to be applied in all such situations, and indeed in all situations which are 'problems'.

First, realise deeply that the problem part of the situation is in your mind and in your mind only. The facts are the facts; it is only to you that they are a problem. *You* have made the problem; that is why only you can solve it. Now be truthful with yourself. What part of you made the problem as such? The answer is surely clear, the lower you or self. Remove that factor and you will generally find there is no problem left. You know quite well, I say to you dogmatically, what you ought to do here, but you don't want to do it. There is no problem about which is the right thing to do, once you take self out of it and what *it* wants to do. The same principle applies to the choice of holidays—what you or your wife want—or to being faithful to your wife or not! Remove self from the mess with a pair of tweezers, and the knot, so to speak, falls to pieces as such and is just a piece of string.

Having faced the fact that the problem is only in your mind, and that it is only self that made it, it is surely not so difficult. A far more complex situation arises when one has to choose between helping this person *or* that, or even of having to hurt this person *or* that. But still, you tied the knot by wrong thinking or wrong action, and only you can unravel it, in your mind. Does this help? Of course it does, for I am only telling you that there is no problem, and what you need is the guts to do what you know to be right. There I cannot help you, but only hope I shall never have to produce the guts to do what you have to do, and to do here and now, with dignity and no ill will.

Good solving,
Yours in the battle,

To the Zen Class:

So we come to the end of another year, and for most of us it has been a year of visible progress. But before we part for the holidays may I make a distinction, to clarify what seems to be a growing confusion, that between Zen and the Zen school. Zen is the Absolute, nothing less, and Zen experience is experience of the Absolute while in bodily form. As such, it can have no boundaries, and is of the East and West as of North and South in any corner of the universe. The Zen school of Buddhism, founded in China but now principally to be found in Korea and Japan, is a group of persons of one religion, Buddhism, who by a special and unique tradition and technique, strive to develop their inner faculties to the point when they will attain, at first in flashes and then at will, that Zen experience. The Buddha did not found Buddhism; that was the work of his followers. Nor did Bodhidharma found Zen. No Teacher founds a sect or school of religion. He teaches Truth as he sees it—what he sees of Truth. His followers, unable to receive this Truth on the plane on which it was given, drag it down, as a dog drags a bone off the table, in order to digest it at leisure on the lower plane of the intellect. The relation, then, of Zen Buddhism to Zen is that of a candle to the sun. Followers of the Nichiren sect of Japan concentrate on one Scripture, the Saddharmapundarika, to the exclusion of all else. In the same way certain of the Theravada school today are concentrating exclusively on the Satipatthana Sutra of the Pali Canon. Let them do so, but they must not call the view in front of them Buddhism. Their blinkers are too narrow, whereas the Buddha, and perhaps only he, wore none at all. So with Zen; it knows no boundaries, no scriptures, no specialised technique. It *is*, and it is for us to find it, in our own minds, which are part of All-Mind, which is No-Mind.

Now teach. Teach to those who know still less than you those principles which may bring light into their darkness. Let me quote from the book I happen to be reading for the seventh or eight time. 'Men seek after knowledge', says the Master K. H. to A. P. Sinnett, 'until they weary themselves to death, but even they do not feel very impatient to help their neighbour with their knowledge; hence there arises a coldness, a mutual indifference which renders him *who knows* inconsistent with himself and inharmonious with his surroundings.' Blood should circulate; stagnant, it goes bad and poisons the body that once kept it alive. So with knowledge of the principles of Truth. What you know, hand on. Into the vacuum thus created life will flow with more intensity. Only a void can successfully demand to be filled. 'Give and it shall be given unto you' is, like so much else in the New Testament, magnificently true. And even on the lowest plane, the effort to formulate clearly what you think you know will help you to understand your own knowledge. One has to understand very thoroughly and deeply before one can teach simply. Try, and you will see what I mean, as I, by such means, am perpetually made aware of how very little I know.

CHAPTER VI

CONCENTRATION AND MEDITATION

From Talks to the Meditation Class of the Buddhist Society, 1930-39
and to the Zen Class, 1952-59.

The subject of Concentration and Meditation is enormous and
no attempt is here made to cover it. My purpose is to concentrate
on Zen meditation, not only as practised in Japan but as most
suitable for the West. For the subject as a whole I recommend
Concentration and Meditation, which was compiled with the help
of the Meditation Circle between 1932 and 1934 and published by
the Society in 1935. It has been in print ever since and is now
published by John Watkins. For Zen meditation consult Dr
Suzuki's works, and in particular *The Training of the Zen Buddhist
Monk* and his *Manual of Zen Buddhism*. For the Scriptures most
used in Zen monasteries see Dr Edward Conze's *Buddhist Wisdom
Books*, the *Sutra of Hui-neng* (Wei Lang) and John Blofeld's *Zen
Teaching of Huang-Po*. Other useful works are Professor Ogata's
Zen for the West and perhaps Chapter Eleven of my own *Zen
Buddhism*.

I have treated the subject in two parts: Part One, Concentration
and Meditation, and the great distinction between them as I use
those terms; and Part Two, a consideration of the fascinating but
tricky subject of 'every minute Zen', or 'Usual life is very Tao',
and the doctrine of Here, Now and This.

But first some basic principles, without understanding which the
beginner will do far worse than waste his time. For the mind is the
world's most powerful engine, and even as one does not allow a
child to pull levers in a power-house 'to see what happens', so the

wise beginner knows what he is doing and why, before he tries to do it.

1.   *Meditation is necessary*

The more the Western mind is subject daily to physical, emotional and mental stress in the very task of keeping alive, the more is it necessary to spend some time, daily if possible, in drawing on the deeps of our innate wisdom, strength and serenity, in aligning the part with the Whole, in returning 'home' for comfort, strength and peace. From moving at the edge of the circle we need the 'still centre of the turning world'; from peripheral fog, the dust of the market place or the darkness of unlit illusion, we need to lift our heads into the Light; from the exhausting heat of the 'three fires' of hatred, lust and illusion, we need periods of self-mastery and that peace which lies at the other end of desire.

But the occasional 'return home' is insufficient. Even flashes of what we are pleased to call direct experience are only indications of a movement in the right direction. The total development of that complex entity, man, is a task of many lives, and though learning and morality have their place in that process, sooner or later the enormous task of the mind's development must be planned, and begun, and unceasingly continued. In this great enterprise I have formulated two good rules, Begin, and Walk On!

In the ideal, and it is a very far ideal, it will be enough to 'meditate', whatever that may mean, at every moment of the daily round. I do not say that this is impossible. I do say that I have never met a man who could do it. True, we can and shall increasingly infuse the deed of the moment with the spirit of Zen, but that, well done, is the product of long mental training, produced in the 'soul's gymnasium' of the meditation hour.

Meditation, in brief, must pass from the phase of an interesting hobby to that of a valued amenity, and thence to a necessity. When the art and craft is mastered there will be time for it to be applied.

2.   *Why meditate?*

Before taking on any new enterprise it is well to ask oneself, Why? The answers can be many, and all are selfish or unselfish, with results accordingly. To develop the mind in order to develop 'powers' is at all times folly, and generally what is popularly called 'black magic', that is, the abuse of spiritual powers to selfish ends. That way lies suffering untold, madness and spiritual death. The only right answer is to fit oneself the better for the service of mankind, whether immediately, as in the Bodhisattva ideal, or in due course, when one's own development is well-progressed, as in the Arhat ideal. But the dedication must be thorough, irrevocable and frequently confirmed. On the Path to Nirvana 'the first step is to live to benefit mankind', and the sooner the would-be pilgrim on that Road is steeped in that great truth, the better for his salvation.

Why, then, do *you* want to learn to meditate, and thereafter to practise it? Because it is the latest 'fashion', or to run away from your problems, or to develop powers that will make you superior to your neighbour? Or to increase your capacity to serve? To achieve a serenity, certainty and sense of oneness with all life which will prepare the mind for Satori and all that lies beyond? Yet even this is not the right reason, though for the time being it is good enough. The utterly right reason will arrive in meditation. Meanwhile, as Hui-neng told us, 'to meditate is to realise inwardly the imperturbability of the Essence of Mind'.

3. *Are you fit?*

Are you physically fit enough to breathe deeply and regularly, to sit still for a quarter of an hour or longer at a time? Do you sleep well, to recuperate from the extra effort on the brain? As for 'pure' living, bear in mind what you are trying to do. Towards the end of the journey you will have to give up all meat, all alcohol, all drugs, whether tobacco, tea or coffee, all sexual indulgence of any kind and even contact with other humans. But to do this at once will make you very sensitive, and psychically sensitive, so that life in the crowded, filthy psychic atmosphere of our cities will be repulsive and almost impossible. Of these indulgences of the self meat-eating produces the greatest problem. On the one hand, it is cruel at our stage of evolution to be party to the killing of other mammals for our food; on the other hand, it is not easy in City life to get enough to eat of other forms of protein without producing the fat and pasty appearance which was at one time almost synonymous with vegetarianism. In these conditions one can only work out one's own 'right' way at the time. For myself I confess to the view that there are more important ways of spending time and mental energy than in troubling about what one eats, and I am certain that the ancient teaching is right that a false belief is a far greater obstacle on the road to enlightenment than a host of misbehaviour on the physical plane. For the rest, the rule is moderation and common-sense.

Are you emotionally fit? The man in love, the man pursuing a vendetta, the man full of troubles, worries, hates, and fears, is not yet in a condition to concentrate, much less to meditate with any hope of success. Are you mentally balanced? If beset with complexes, projections, violent views; if aggressive to all differing opinion, fixed in your conclusions; or the reverse, too timid to hold any views at all lest someone of a stronger mind cry 'Boo' to you, then wait. The development of the mind must rise from sure foundations, and as the building rises any latent faults and cracks may bring it tottering to the ground. Cracks in the mind should be found and healed before meditation is undertaken; later, the crack may widen and split the mind.

4. *Only methods can be taught*
Work out your own salvation, said the All-Enlightened One, and this is the heart of 'Buddhism'. No books, no lectures, not the greatest master in the world can do one hour of the work for you. All these are fingers pointing to the moon. *You* must do the work, and all of it, and would that all of you had already learnt this lesson, which is probably the most difficult of all to learn. The amount of ingenuity exercised by the human mind in getting someone else to do its spiritual labour is staggering, and we are all still trying! Methods are endless in their variety, and more are being invented day by day. But all have this in common, that one must begin, and one must continue. The effort will produce its stress and strain; there will be difficulties innumerable, and adventures grave and gay upon the Road. But whatever the method chosen, the pupil and the pupil alone must produce an inexhaustible supply of 'guts' to keep him moving on the Way.

5. *Common sense is needed all the time*
There is nothing mysterious about meditation, nothing holy, or occult. But in the early stages new habits are being created, new channels in the stubborn mind deliberately dug and widened.

As in the development of new muscles there must be patience and persistence, regular practice but never too much. It is useless to begin with three hours a day, as it is foolish to attempt to develop biceps with three hours' work on the first day with the dumb-bells. At first there will be a struggle with the mind; then the new habits will be formed, and the practice will become a habit as much as shaving or doing the hair; then the habit will become a necessity, and the most longed-for hour of the day. There will be no quick results worth having, nor should the eyes be looking for them. But there *will* be results, pleasant and unpleasant, and in time the joys of hard-won achievement, in which the teacher, if any, will take some pride but claim no share.

6. *The whole man is involved*
The self, the Self, and the SELF, all these are one, and aspects of one unity. The whole man climbs, and takes his muddy boots to the summit of his spiritual Everest. The self is called the 'shadow' in modern psychology, but a shadow needs an object to cast it and a light. The object is the Self, the growing, evolving something which moves to Enlightenment. The light that throws the shadow is the SELF, the Light which is not yours or mine but the one Light born of the Darkness of the unborn Universe. The shadow must die, fade, become no more; so must the Self in time, leaving but the Essence of Mind which is All-Mind, which is No-Mind. Meanwhile, take your boots with you, cleaning them at times.

7. *The immediate purpose should be clear*
Fix the immediate goal and reach it; there is time then to reach further. There is too much vague and hindering talk of the nature of Satori, or the comparative value of this and that 'experience'. There will be time enough to discuss the view from the mountain top when you get there. For most of us the Goal can be the One; there will be time enough to discuss what lies beyond when we have achieved so far. While none of us has yet achieved the One does it matter *what* is neither One nor two? Let us be modest in immediate purpose, enormous only in our 'spirit of enquiry' and our insatiable will to achieve.

8. *Concentration versus Meditation*

I use this word versus to emphasize the profound distinction between these two uses of the mind. By Concentration I mean the deliberate creation or development of the mental faculty of focusing consciousness at will on a chosen object. It is the forging of the instrument, the cutting of the tool, the development of the special muscles needed for a special job. It is the building of the car which a driver will drive where he will, the creation of a searchlight which, under the technician's hand, will focus as directed, for as long as directed, and can then be switched elsewhere or switched off. By Meditation I mean the deliberate use of this instrument to a chosen end. There can be no meditation of value until the mind used is under the control of the will. Before the dancer is permitted to dance she practises for months and years at the *barre*; before the engineer attempts to build up a bridge he spends long years on learning the necessities of his science. I am pressing this point because too many would-be meditators are quite incapable of Concentration of the type needed, and far too lazy to learn.

So to *Concentration*. First, it is a faculty used every day by every human being who is not an idiot. Children concentrate fiercely on their toys, or the television; an audience watches, with full attention, a play, a street accident or royalty. This is not in the least spiritual, but that selectivity of attention which is necessary for efficiency in any job, from sharpening a pencil to making war. Here there is no effort to exclude other interests from the field of attention for there is little or no energy left to focus elsewhere. The searchlight has picked out the church steeple or the enemy plane, and outside its beam there is the darkness of complete disinterest. But, and the distinction is considerable, all the usual examples of concentration have this in common, that the object is holding the subject's attention, emotionally or mentally; the pull is from the object end of the piece of elastic; hence such phrases as 'My attention was held by . . .', 'I was spell-bound, fascinated . . . I could not tear my eyes away.' Now the process must be reversed. In cold blood the subject, which is you, must decide the object, even against desire for something else, active dislike of the object, or at least boredom and resentment at the exercise. The object now may be the door-knob, or abstract, such as the relation between devotion and pity, or with no meaning at all, like a koan. Now comes the rub, indeed the enormous problem, how to exclude from this chosen field the host of thoughts, emotions and desires which will fight, as though with a life of their own, to enter the roped-off field. This problem is so large that famous scriptures give it their whole attention. The opening sentence of Patanjali's famous *Yoga Aphorisms* may be translated, 'Yoga is the hindrance of the modifications of the thinking principle', or in simpler English, is the power to stop the mind from running about. How this is accomplished is, like so much else, a matter of choice of method, and comes under the large heading of 'skill in means' (*upaya kausalyana*), of which so much is said in Mahayana literature. Some fight the intruders; others welcome them, examine them and let them go; others just ignore them. But sooner or later, by one means or another, control is gained. Then, and only then, is the pupil ready to begin to meditate, to use his trained and obedient instrument to do what he wants to do. Now the car is ready to be driven, the dancer ready to interpret, with a perfectly controlled body, the subtleties of Giselle. This does not mean that Meditation is banned during the years necessary for the training of the mind in Concentration, but what is the use of attempting to hit the bull's eye when you cannot draw the bow, of composing a symphony when you don't know a sharp from a flat? But given this new power of selectivity of wave-length, of focusing the whole power of the mind as you will, for as long as you will, until you decide to switch it off—you may usefully and successfully meditate.

9. *And so to Meditation*

Again consider the purpose of meditation and see that the motive is at all times pure. For now the meditator enters the field of 'spiritual' forces. The term is of course comparative, for there is nothing completely spiritual or material that we know. But these 'higher' forces, as yet unknown to science and to all but a few psychologists, are immensely powerful, and have their own laws. Never should a claim be made to their possession, nor should they be unnecessarily displayed or money taken for their use. To abuse the possession of greater wisdom, strength or power of mind is utterly evil, and even to keep it for oneself alone is, according to tradition, that which distinguishes the Pratyeka Buddha from the

Buddhas of Infinite Compassion, of whom Gautama was in history the one we know.

It is now more necessary for a regular time to be observed when the meditator can keep himself apart. This is to make it easier to protect the mind from interference, but also the body, for in deep meditation a sudden shock to the body can produce headaches, palpitation and the like. If such a place cannot be found in the home, the nearest Church will do nicely. As to time, let it be early or late, but the earlier in the day the better, for the whole being is fresher and the earth current is a rising rather than a falling tide. But it is more important for the time to be regular than to aim at any particular time. The mind creates its own habits, and like the animals at the Zoo at their feeding time, will be ready for its spiritual meal.

As to posture I have firm ideas. I do not doubt that the full 'lotus' posture is the ideal, and next to that the ordinary cross-legged position known to all small boys. But I am equally convinced that for a long way on the Way there is no need for such a posture, so long as the head and spine be kept erect and the circuit closed. Let those who can sit comfortably on the floor in the traditional Buddhist posture do so, with the seat itself a few inches higher than the ankles. Let others sit as they will, erect and yet relaxed, and with the muscles balanced so that breathing is easy and regular and the body can so sit for half an hour without any movement at all. The 'circuit' should be closed by folding the hands and in some way closing the feet together. The whole 'Self' is, on several planes, a powerful generator of the force which in one of its forms we call electricity. Let the induced pressure be conserved and not dissipated from carelessly 'earthed' hands and feet. I do not myself approve the eyes half-open, as I believe that it tends to induce a fixed stare which is bad for the eyes. Even if the eyes being closed induces sleep, does that matter? When you wake you begin again. Personally I can happily meditate in a train or even a bus, but I agree one may with ease go past one's station!

The theme for meditation is for a long while immaterial. The breath itself can be used, and is perhaps the oldest of all. But use the breath just as you breathe, and without the Indian Yogic exercise of fancy breathing which can, when not supervised by a very skilful teacher, lead to the most serious results. I repeat, you are now developing and hoping to control the most powerful machine in the whole world, the human mind. Don't play the fool with it.

But whatever the theme, breathing, a phrase, a concept, it is better at first to begin with a few minutes 'warming up' exercises. Some watch the breathing, some take Pansil, some 'pass through the bodies' as I have shown you, discarding the body, the emotions, the thoughts, till nought is left but the silence or the white Light or whatever device you choose. For all these methods are devices; all are right for some at some time; none is right for all, or for anyone all the time.

But now you are going deeper, or higher, however you think of these things. You are withdrawing from the edge of existence to its centre, moving higher above the world of men into that of the Enlightened Ones. You are raising consciousness above its habitual level to one less immersed in the unreal self or 'you', more free of the stains of hatred, lust and illusion, more that of the Self, the higher Self in the sense that we have agreed to use that term. The Goal, remember, is Non-duality and nothing less, and the last thought of feeling of self must die before that moment of awareness can be attained.

At the end of the period, long or short, come gently back to 'reality', trying to preserve the link with Reality as long as possible. Then share your treasure with all mankind. Use the four Brahma Viharas to send your love and compassion and joy and equanimity to all that lives, above, below and everywhere. This helps to reduce the risk of an inflated ego, empties the unreal self, thus making room for the Life and Joy of the universe to enter in, and ensures that your period of time thus spent has been of some use to mankind.

From theme to theme, from meditation with 'seed' to that with 'no seed'. Let us be practical—and modest. When we have learned to concentrate, and to meditate with seed, i.e. with a theme or chosen object, there will be time enough to go further, and you will not need these notes. Therefore I say nothing of Contemplation, nor do I speak of the subtle distinctions between Samadhi, Dhyana, Prajna and the like. What gross immodesty for us to discuss them! Do we argue the niceties of the last stage on Everest as we stroll up Hampstead Heath?

But this we must watch, that we do not leave the road. This

Middle Way is infinitely narrow, and the blind alleys and worse to either side are infinite in number. Beware of trance conditions, from naked self-hypnosis to the subtlest and 'most enjoyable' condition of lotus-eating peace. The difference is that of a flash of lightning to the warm glow of an electric stove. He who touches the fringe of the Absolute *knows* and does not talk of it.

The faculty by which this true experience will be gained is Buddhi, the intuition, and this is far beyond the most pleasant condition of high-thought repose—as of any trance of any kind. The right attitude for meditation is perfectly balanced between the opposites, positive/negative, alert/relaxed, receiving/giving, one with all. Beware of revolving like the proverbial squirrel in the thought-machine. You are still going round on the Wheel of Becoming, and Satori lies at right-angles, it has been said, to the plane of that Wheel.

10. *Zen Meditation*

The foregoing applies, I believe, to all meditation. What is there special about Zen? Only the precise definition of its object—Satori, and nothing less. But the Rinzai and the Soto schools use very different methods to this end. Rinzai, which we know in the West through the writings of Dr Suzuki, Professor Ogata and those who have learnt their Zen from them, is short, and fierce, and sudden. It is also boisterous and joyous and enormous fun. It is ferociously subtle, nebulous yet certain in attack, indifferent in defeat, and laughing all the time. I will not have it that the school of gentle loving-kindness only is compatible with Rinzai Zen. Rinzai stabs at the balloon of self, tears down every concept and the stillness of serene delight. It hacks at thought as a desperate man cuts down the jungle to escape from it; it lives intensely in the Here and Now and This.

Soto Zen, I understand, though it is not easy to get information beyond the merest platitude, eschews the *koan* and *mondo* beloved of Rinzai Zen, is far more gentle, feminine, introvert and con-templative—as many of you, who have but doubtful place in a Rinzai circle. For the latter ignores the Bhakti element of mystical devotion, and some of you miss it. It is desperately direct, and therefore impatient of any moment spent in anything less than the direct assault on Reality.

The Zen Class of the Buddhist Society aims at such a goal, and its members look to find it. You appreciate the value of an agreed self-discipline, for the paradox stands that only he who is self-controlled is free. But gentle browsing in the mind will not produce those 'moments' which are out of time. The effort must be continuous and considerable. The 'Great Spirit of Enquiry' must be backed by a trained and indomitable will. Even as those who fight with naked swords, even as a man whose head is held under water fights for air, so must the man of Zen be fighting all the time for Enlightenment. True, there are those who seem serene and simple, gentle and at peace—*now*, but this is the reward of achievement, the sign that the battle is over, and largely won. For us there is the need of im-mediate urgency. The form of that fighting is for each to decide; meanwhile we are trying to fight together, in the sense of side by side.

11. *Group Meditation*

Members of a meditation group should be, in the old phrase, 'as the fingers of one hand'. Any gossip or ill-will at personality level makes smooth and efficient work at higher levels of consciousness impossible, and the damage done by one person indulging in such can be remarkable. The teacher or leader must be respected, but in Western lands no more than respected. The devotion accorded a true teacher in the more devotional East is too apt in the West to degenerate into a psychological transference, with embarrassment to the teacher and stoppage of all development for the pupil. The pupils in a group, as elsewhere, must learn to stand on their own two feet, and not on the teacher's, and he serves them ill if he does not assist them to do so. When for any reason the leader considers a particular member can benefit no more from membership of the group, he must be allowed to say so. In the same way a pupil can leave when he will. But in either case the parting should be serene and dignified.

12. *And so to Results*

It is cold truth that results should not be sought, at least too strenuously. Just as Kipling was right in saying that 'the Race is run by one and one, and never by two and two', so he was right in saying, 'The Game is more than the player of the game, and the

Ship is more than the crew.' The team, be it group or some greater Brotherhood, must be ever served, and the team that needs all our help all the time is mankind. Results for the individual are only of value to the extent that they serve that end. But they will come. The wise man is concerned with causes, seldom with effects. If the work is right, and carried out without pause, results, and the right results, *must* come. The inner effects are what matters to true spiritual development, and these may not appear for a long while to one's friends. The felt effects will come in time, serenity, certainty, and greater ability to 'cope'. Meanwhile, it is wise to forget results in the playing of the game for the sake of the game, following right, as Tennyson would say, 'in the scorn of consequence'. The Bodhisattva vows, never to take the reward that is earned until the last blade of grass has entered Buddhahood, will save the ego from its pride, and these vows are daily recited in Zen monasteries. Meanwhile begin, and then continue. I know of little in all the literature of meditation that says more. And the only equipment for the journey that I have found of value is this—right Motive, right Modesty, and unlimited Guts!

13. *'Every Minute' Meditation*

In one sense the whole work of the Zen Class is dedicated to this end, and there is therefore little to be said. Twice you have considered the subject in the Questions set you, and we have it well in mind that in Buddhism, as distinct from other 'religions', the great Supreme, with plenty of capital letters, is not the end of spiritual effort, or even its main purpose. In the famous ten Ox-herding Pictures (see Dr Suzuki's *Manual of Zen Buddhism*), at the 8th stage both Ox and Man have gone out of sight, and the picture is a blank circle. But Picture 9 is 'Back to the Source', a state of habitual consciousness which is neither in Satori nor out of it; then comes the last Picture, 'Entering the City with Bliss-bestowing Hands'. In other words, back to the grindstone, in the office or the home or the market-place. Thereafter the all-but Sage is 'in the world but not of it'. He wears the Yellow Robe internally, in W. Q. Judge's great phrase; he is, whatever else he is doing, meditating all the time. In the end this is the only form of meditation needful, but it is a high stage of development and must, like all else, be patiently attained. No sudden flash of intuitive understanding

154

will produce this faculty, for the whole man is harnessed by it, and the wholeness is an integration of many lives.

How do we best approach this ultimate faculty, of living the spiritual life in the material, of achieving 'a devotion to minute, holy things from the saving of a pin to a healing meditation', as one of you put it? How to 'infuse an active life with Zen, to do it all the time —and not to reserve one's Zen (as brandy) only for crises and best occasions', as another wrote? There seem to be two main ways, and they are not alternative. One is to leave the infusion to the unconscious, so to deepen and prolong one's periods of inturned meditation that the mind can be left to produce the flower of that practice in daily life. The other is to work consciously towards this spiritual infusion, allowing for periods of reaction, and avoiding the danger of becoming a spiritual snob.

This conscious practice can begin with the present discipline of an act of awareness, focused on the Society's Shrine at 12, 6 and 9 p.m. Let this be expanded to every time the clock strikes the hour, the half hour, the quarter . . . Then have the phrase belonging to the fortnightly period truly 'at the front of the back of the mind' as someone called it, that is, ready to enter and fully occupy the mind the moment there is nothing else which has to be given priority. This habit, once formed—and all this is a matter of habit-formation—can itself present a profound change in the personality, perhaps too profound to leave life comfortable with one's neighbours and friends. The person concerned will be found to be 'pre-occupied' with other thoughts. So he is—giving these more worth-while thoughts priority over chatter, drivel and gossip. For a change, use the text-book in the pocket or purse. One can mull over the *Dhammapada*, *Voice of the Silence*, *Bhagavad Gita*, *Hui-neng* or what you please for years on end, and all these and more are available in pocket editions.

It is helpful, and if I may mount my hobby-horse, or one of the most mettlesome, *necessary* to learn to teach—if only as a useful way of learning. Imagine yourself, if it is not yet true, preparing for a talk, an article, or at least a contribution to a discussion on some theme, or the theme in hand; work out what you have to say, in outline and in actual phrases, to make it clear to the humblest enquirer. This is active, positive, dynamic thinking, creating new forms of old truths. Imagine a friend suddenly asking you, 'What is the doctrine of Karma . . . of Self-reliance without a God? What is Zen compared with mystical Christianity? What *is* Zen?' Are you ready to answer? Why not?

And so the mind is trained to face and solve the manifold problems and 'difficult' situations of daily life. This faculty of facing and becoming one with innumerable situations is part of the training in Zen adopted in Japan. The situation may be a minor domestic difficulty, or the impossible ones described in Zen writings, as in the 5th of the Mumonkwan (see Ogata's *Zen for the West*, p. 97). But all these problems have much in common, in their nature and treatment. First, they are all mind-made; the problem is not in the situation but in the mind of the man who makes of those factors a problem which he has to solve. Secondly, in every problem troubling one as such, there is the factor of self involved; by abstracting it the problem is in most cases solved, that is, it is seen that there was no problem save the interference of personal desire. Say to yourself, what do 'I' want here? Remove that factor, and is there a problem left? What remains is often the need to *do* what you now see clearly to be the only right thing to do! Thirdly, where there is a genuine choice to be made between two duties or two ways of helping, it is safe to choose that which the more directly leads to oneness, integration, wholeness—Non-duality. And fourthly, of a hundred things which must be said, attempt to raise consciousness above the tension of the two horns of the dilemma. From that viewpoint the solution may be obvious or, as the man at the second floor window who may be in sunlight, and listen, though with troubled mind, to the car-drivers hooting at each other in the ground-level fog, there may be for him no problem.

But once it is decided what is the right action, let it be done, firmly, directly and impersonally, and let the consequences, pleasant or unpleasant, be taken as they come.

One can use in meditation phrases deliberately chosen to help the mind in daily life. The mystical yet dynamic awareness of the sole Reality of the Essence of Mind, and the illusion of all else; the fact that we *are* all enlightened, as the Patriarch Hui-neng proclaimed, and only differ in our ability to know it; the advice of *The Voice of Silence*, 'Look within—thou *art* Buddha.' These truths are true; practise making them so.

Thus the practice of Here, Now and This will grow. I have told it you many times, and here will but repeat it briefly. There is nowhere for you but Here. In an hour's time you may be somewhere else; you will still be Here (though it may be a new 'here'). It is always Now, and will be Now tomorrow as it was Now yesterday. And you can only be concerned with This, what you are concerned with Now and Here. All else is memory or imagination, memory of the non-existent Past or imagination of the non-existent Future. And Now? How long is Now? In one sense no length at all, for a millionth of a second ago is Past, and a millionth ahead is not yet come. So only the Now exists, the timeless, cosmic, everlasting Now, of Eckhart and a score of Western mystics, and of Suzuki and all those of the East. Thus there is nothing else which can occupy your mind than This, but you can decide very often what This shall be. It is always the product of your karmic past, and is not less holy for being manure to be put on the compost heap, or more so for being incense for the Shrine.

It will come! The practice of 'every minute' Zen will come, but it will take time as we use that term, and call for much patience. Difficulties will dissolve, distinctions blend and blur. You will be the more able to cope with all that life may bring to you, and see the terms good and bad, and pleasant and unpleasant, and other pairs of the opposites, as labels you attach to circumstance. Your friends will be less your friends in that you have less need of them; your enemies have less power to wound as that which alone they can injure, self, begins to fade away. Past and future will less tangle you with memories or hope. You will stand the more firmly on your own two feet, and walk on them happily to the (non-existent) Goal. You may even find the truth in the *mondo* which dominates this section of my talk. Nansen was once asked by Jyoshu, 'What is Tao?' Said Nansen, 'Ordinary mind is Tao'. Said Jyoshu, 'Should we try to attain it?'. 'If you try to attain it you will fail', said Nansen. Mumon's comment is to the point. 'Even though Jyoshu was immediately enlightened, he will reach that state for the first time after studying Zen for more than thirty years.' Carry on.

CHAPTER VII

THE APPROACH TO ZEN

Dear Mrs Mansfield,

As you could not attend the series of talks on 'Every Minute Zen' I am answering your letter as to coping with situations as they arise. As I was told long ago, one of the main purposes of Zen training is to fit the pupil to cope with any situation at any time. Hence, no doubt, by way of training, the 'impossible situations' described, for example, in the *Mumonkwan* where the man is hanging over the precipice by his teeth, or Nansen holding up the cat in order to *create* such a violent situation—(see Ogata's *Zen for the West* Appendix I), and W. J. Gabb made much in his own *The Goose is Out* of 'The Address to the Situation'. Professor Ogata at the 1957 Summer School invented a situation to get our reaction to it, and life is certainly presenting them every day. How can we train ourselves to the 'right' reaction to these situations? I think we can do it, but here as always I can but offer the principles which work in my own case and may work in yours.

The task, in modern terminology, is one of adjustment, to people and to circumstance. The ideally balanced man is neither aggressive nor shy, neither wanting anything from the situation for himself, nor resenting its possession by others. He is unattached but not indifferent, balanced between the opposites of introversion and extraversion, and seeing the inside and the outside as two sides of a coin.

All this is easy to say but hard to use. For it implies a considerable degree of emotional maturity. The man capable of coping with any crises must have his emotions under remarkable control, which implies that he has no 'feelings' to get hurt, and indeed cannot be hurt by anything which another does or says. It implies also a mental stability which is all too rare. On the one hand there must be no will to impose one's own decision and desires onto the knot of circumstance; on the other, no running away, an acceptance of all that is because it *is*, and a willingness to help, as seems right, in any way. All this is a matter of balance, standing on our own feet and not on our neighbour's, and not leaning on any teacher or Master or God. In a crowd or in the desert, facing an angry employer or a proposal of marriage, a difficult Board Meeting or a row in the kitchen, the stance should be that of the boxer or the swordsman, or the man of Judo—poised, alert, tense yet relaxed, one-pointed on the situation yet desiring nothing at all.

This brings in the Zen technique of no-technique. The faculty for problem-solving is the intuition, and the state of mind, No-mind. How? To find the Way to a mountain top, go to the top and look for it. How to get the goose out of the bottle? 'There, it's out'. But this is easy to say. When we achieve the summit we need not seek for it. Meanwhile we have to cope with situations and each other in the world of duality, often in a hurry, and in the bustle and noise of the market-place. At the moment we can but improve our ability to cope; perfection is the fruit of long self-discipline and practice in the final art, the art of living.

How to prepare the mind deliberately to cope? We can keep it high. The level or plane on which it operates is a matter of habit. We can keep the level, in work and play, fooling and recreation, at least unhurtful, at least not adding more than we need to the fires of hatred, lust and illusion that cloud the Light that shines eternally within. We can keep it open to the intuition, obeying the small voice of its promptings, and in all things, so far as that lovely ideal is possible, 'letting the mind abide nowhere', in opinion, conviction or logical conclusion, but letting it fly free, as a bird that feels the sun and the wind and the rain and knows them to be one.

For in the end the situation is mind-made, and it is one with the viewer. So long as there is the man to cope and the thing to be coped with there are two things and not one; there must be tension, the old tension between the 'opposites.' Until the subject (you) and the situation (the object) are one, 'you' cannot cope, i.e. there will be no coping. Only when you learn the trick of at-oneing yourself with the problem can you just walk through it as if it were not there. Wrap yourself up in it, eat it, digest it, and forget it; do anything but don't look at it with the eyes of a beholder and wonder what to do *about* it. *There is only one thing-you-problem.* It is not *you-in*-problem, like bird-in-cage, but a oneness in which the only trouble is that you *will* regard it as two!

Your action may be fierce and immediate; or it may be doing just nothing at all (which is often a very powerful form of action); it may be that delicate variation and alternation of push-let go-push-let go, like an English Police Officer with a large and peevish crowd. He moves a thousand where he wills without fuss, effort, or the least doubt of his ability to do so. Try coping with a crowd pouring out of a train when you want to move against them. Don't push-keep ice-cold; just move, a little here, a step there and, if you are skilful, like the butcher with his knife in Chuang-Tze, you will bump no-one but quite soon arrive.

Meanwhile, just look at the next 'difficult situation' with a bored and placid eye, and *eat it*.

Yours (having coped with *that* situation, or have I?),

LETTER 73

Dear Martha,

Why be so bashful about acquiring merit? You do, whether you will or no, until you come to that stage when each act of good is so impersonal that no 'self' exists to take the beneficial consequences. And that is far off for us yet. If Karma be true, the effects of our causes come back to us, for 'good' or 'ill' according as we label them. It follows that the 'reservoir' of good of a well-doing man becomes considerable, and as all is one that reservoir increases the bank of good available to all. In time, as the doer of good is less and less attached to the results of his well-doing, he can direct it, that is, make it available as and where he will, for healing, strengthening and enlightening others. But he must learn to conserve his strength thus acquired, and on all planes. Physically, he will not waste energy; on the psychic plane he will conserve the enormous power of sex, which is dissipated in sexual discharge; emotionally he is calm and self-collected, and does not heat the very atmosphere around him with incessant bursts of love, hate, fear, jealousy and general excitement; mentally he forms no opinions, makes no decisions, transfers no criticism unless called on to do so. And in the spiritual field he wastes no force at all. To the extent he succeeds in this high ideal he is a dynamo of enormous power, able to draw on huge reserves of strength as needed. And merit is such strength. It is only the good action done with the *intent* to acquire merit that is so much less a good action. We may laugh at those in the East who build a pagoda, pay for the printing of a Buddhist book, or even found a hospital, *in order* to acquire merit, but are we free from the same weakness? One test is the extent to which we are indifferent to thanks when we have done good. If we are secretly annoyed at not being thanked, is it that we wanted to be sure that the merit of the deed was safely banked?

Meanwhile we are not yet beyond suffering, in the sense of bearing, the results of our thoughts and deeds. And until we attain satori we need that reservoir of strength, every ounce of it, to work up the 'head of steam', as Tom calls it, which alone will enable the one-pointed ferociously-determined mind to break through to Enlightenment. True, the force is not ours but that of the Universe—there is but one Force, but the efforts of the puny part have accumulated the momentum which will carry the fighter through the mind-barrier to No-Mind. So go on acquiring merit, and you know the way to gather the most in the minimum of time? By giving it away as fast as you get it, by offering it, and the fruits of every act *before you do it*, to all mankind. Try it. For 'if the first step is to live to benefit mankind', it is also the last.

Yours, in the union of merit,

LETTER 74

Dear Silver,

Don't over-do the analysis of self, spell it how you will. More important than any analysis is the fact that there is only one SELF, and each Self and equally each self, the shadow of the Self, is all one. It is one in each 'unit', so to speak, that we know as a man with a name and address, and it is one with the All-Mind, or No-Mind, or Absolute Mind which is All. Get these truths into your head as plain simple facts, and not merely sentimentally spiritual ideals with a row of capital letters, and you will see the meaning of *meta*-physics, and of that *meta*-Science to which science as yet pays no regard. In Class we have found that as each 'unit' moves up its consciousness to function more and more at the level of Self, it becomes more sensitive to those about it. Unfortunately, some find that they begin by becoming more sensitive to each other's *personalities*; hence unpleasant jealousies and spiteful gossip. But as these lumps and bumps get rubbed off in class relationship the inner development opens, and the sense of profound unity transcends the friction of the personalities. It is this oneness that we need, the synthetic faculty of the mind rather than the analytic, the awareness of oneness in the face of apparent differences. Remember that 'all distinctions are falsely imagined'. That is TRUE! Try to live it, for in that new life is much new splendour and a new-found joy.

Sincerely,

LETTER 75

Dear Rodney,

I take the view, though it may be wrongly, that too much ink has been spilt on this question of Gradual and Sudden. I see that historically it was of importance to stress the sudden nature of true Enlightenment, but surely we of the Rinzai school of Zen appreciate that both are true. The actual 'moment' of Enlightenment *must* be sudden in terms of time, for it is the transition from the relative to the Absolute, and between those two there is not, nor can there ever be a bridge. There is no neutral point between the opposites as at dawn between night and day. This is the world of duality and *this . . . but there is none who is aware of this which is Absolute*; only when back in relativity can we say . . . or can we say anything or do anything but smile? But the *approach* to this no-moment of Now is and *must* be gradual, that is, step by step, by years and lives of self-training. The experience of satori, as distinct from satori itself, is the result of causes; we have earned that moment and it comes. To that extent we can strive for it, but it is more accurate to say that we strive to be ready for it—'the readiness is all', as Hamlet said. So do not try to solve these cosmic opposites over a cup of tea. Just go direct for what you nakedly and fiercely want, and 'direct' is the key word. The answers to all the rest will in the end appear, where they have always been, in your own mind; but by then you will not trouble to look for them!

Yours suddenly,

LETTER 76

Dear Mary,

Of course all this question of suffering, self and compassion is 'a bit of a muddle', but don't call it 'worrying'. My reason for coming back to it again and again in Class is that with inturned meditation it is all too easy to get 'self'-centred, i.e. to feed the very ego which should be in the throes of death. But if the turning inward is a turning to the common Self in all of us, which is SELF, then no matter, the untrue self is being allowed to die. The danger lies in projecting our self onto things and people and circumstance and letting it stick there. For thus we can see nothing but our own reflection of desire or aversion, or preconception of belief and outworn values, and we see nothing straight and truly at all. In compassion we wake to oneness, and act accordingly. Thereafter it is true to say, as I firmly aver, that no man who is happy has begun to live. And this is in no way dreary and depressing. On the contrary, it is a waking up to facts, cosmic facts, an expansion of consciousness to nothing less than the universe, which is not dreary, but terribly exciting and rather frighteningly true. If all is indeed one, and by now you don't doubt it, then all our joy and suffering is one joy and suffering, though bits of the One, as it were, suffer joy or pain at a particular moment, all exactly apportioned to the causation of that particular part. In this unified field of experience compassion is vastly more than being kind. I tie up my own finger when it is cut; I tie up yours. Why not? They are all fingers of one cosmic hand, so to speak. No, this sense of unity transcends all kindness, or any reason or motive for doing good. Compassion, as I see it, is the waking to cosmic consciousness, the awareness of a tiny light within that is not my light or yours, but the flaming joy in the light of which I see the whole universe. Here is a deep, tremendously deep stirring of consciousness, a sense of being at the heart of a mighty monster which is all creation, and to feel that great heart beating as one's own. In this vast agony and joy there is also serenity; it is Law and Right and it is Good, all of it. All, everything is RIGHT, and yet to make it so we must each of us work our fingers to the bone in deeds, each moment, of kindness and sympathy and healing help.

But you know all this, and I don't know why I am trying to say what I can't say, adequately or at all. But I know that Rightness is the heart of the Buddha-dhamma, and in that rightness is the face of God, our 'original face', and Tao and loveliness and Zen. And self, or Self or SELF? To hell with them all, as concepts. What they are they are, and we shall find them so. Meanwhile I am, though the 'I' expands and shrinks each second of time, according as I get on with the job in hand, or think of me. Yet this isn't true either, for there is no one 'I'. When someone in Class hits the target this 'I' rejoices and shares the reward of joy, and *this* 'I' is jealous and *this* 'I' is bored, having no idea what is happening. It is all one composite, changing, expanding, revolving, self-creating, infinite I, and I AM!

So. Is that clearer? Like mud, you say. Be it so, and get on with your knitting or your boy friend's socks. I care not, for I am about to darn my own, the which I do with exceeding lack of skill, but much delight.

Good darning,

LETTER 77

Dear Brampton,

I am so glad to hear you have 'bored holes in the ceiling' of your roof of thought. It *is* lovely when a ray of light comes in! But if you say you are now ready for the logic of A equals Not-A, 'Zen logic' as Dr Suzuki calls it, it does not follow that I can explain it to you. But it is bound up with 'Why God created the Universe', as Dr Suzuki cheerfully explains, and I will do my best, though briefly.

Take first the (to us) concept of the Absolute. Think, (absurd though it sounds) what absoluteness means. It is both absolute Consciousness and absolute Unconsciousness. It is utterly void of all distinctions. It knows nothing, not even the concept of Nothingness. It *is* but it is nothing—no thing. Next step: To know, it must divide itself; Non-Duality must become Two. Here let me oversimplify, and say that the Absolute becomes Two, though there is, of course, the stage between of One ('All things return to the One. To what does the One return? The answer is—to Non-Duality—the Absolute). Very well. The Absolute becomes One—then Two—and then Three. Why Three? Because no man can even conceive Twoness. Try it. You can conceive One and can easily conceive three, being two things and the relation between them. You can't conceive just two. So what happens? For God to be God he must know that he is God. Agreed? To know that he is God he must divide himself in two so that *something* may know *something other*, the third factor being knowledge, which is their relation. Now you have Knower, Known and Knowledge. God sees and knows himself.

But he pays the price for his knowledge. To know himself as God he must cease to be God; he lessens his Absoluteness by a division which cannot obtain in the Absolute. Therefore, and this is the big jump, to know that he is God he must cease to be God. He *is* God only as he looks at himself as not-God. He becomes God in ceasing to be God. God is God because he is not-God. Are you there? By projecting himself (or a part of himself—but this is quibbling in Theology), yet remaining himself, he is able to see himself and know himself to be—God. Therefore again, he *is* God because and to the extent that he is *not*-God.

Now transfer this to other symbols or ciphers. A is A. Agreed? But A is only A because it is not-A. If A were *only* A it would *not* be A. If A is A it is only *because* A is *not*-A.

Now you see the point of seeking 'your original face'. We must get back, as Dr Suzuki says, behind the moment of division, before there was Two, before God broke himself in two to be God. Only here, in *this* state of consciousness or Mind, which is No-Mind, can we cease to see two as two and see it as One made twofold. In this No-logic, or state of No-Mind, or absence of thought-fetters, we are free of logic, and rationalism, and the world's bondage of 'sense'. We can and do talk Non-Sense, which is super-sense, meta-logic—Truth! Now, and for the first time is the Mind free to 'abide no-where', to alight as it will, but to be snared by no illusion, no projection of self, and to fly away as it will to fresh 'becoming'; thus only will it be free to think, to act, and to be, but from the plane of No-Mind Only! Have we arrived? Here's hoping,

Dear Mrs Wilmer,

I was most interested in your description of moving to a new centre. I think we have to face it that the distinguishing mark of true experience is that we don't know when we are having it—only when we come out. I seem to remember Dr Suzuki saying this of satori, and logically I can see why it must be so. For to know you are having an experience there must be an I to know, and satori, or anything like it, is, above all else, the disappearance for that 'moment' of a self-ish 'I'. When we apply this to states of consciousness, and the centres at which that consciousness functions, there must be a perpetual shift of centre ever nearer to the 'inmost centre in us all, where truth abides in fulness', as Browning calls it. This is 'the still centre of the turning world', but if it is really so we shan't know when we get there! We deliberately shift our centre from self to Self and so on, but then find that a new centre has appeared suddenly from which, for a 'moment', we acted, and are now frantically trying to get back there. The change is an abandonment of the self-centre. As another member wrote to me, 'I am beginning to see how futile are our attempts at "acceptance" or "compassion", or any other qualities we are pleased to think of as virtues—the ego cannot change his spots. What seems to be happening is a change of centre from which one sees the whole world of appearances, *including one's own ego*, which has ceased to be the centre . . . ' I agree with you that the relief from self-pushing pressure is enormous; the serenity in which one can, at these rare periods, move into action, motiveless, 'thought-less', efficient, is lovely, and it must be lovely indeed to pass one's life in that serenity. From that centre questions of Karma, Compassion and Harmony, which we dealt with in one of the sets of Questions, are like bluebottles buzzing; they have no validity at all. There is just the Is-ness of Here and Now and the job to be done and the impersonal doing of it . . . But how to teach it, to get it across, to help others attain? I suppose you are right—one can't, but that does not mean that one does not try!

Yours off-centre till the next moment comes,

LETTER 79

Dear Silver,

Surely you are not still troubled with paradox? All great Teachers have had to use it, partly because it is an exceedingly compressed and striking way of stating the truth, and partly because there is often no other way. 'Give up thy life if thou wouldst live' is paradox, as much as any remark of a Zen Master (if he condescends to stoop to the level of 'sense' in any form). Remember that the Way is a Middle Way, narrow as a razor's edge, and like the analogy of Past, Present and Future, just as neither side exists, so to speak, so is the middle, the Present or any other logically satisfying middle, also an illusion—there is just nothing there! You will agree that if anything is true its opposite is true also. If there is good there must be evil, (see the *Tao Tê Ching* which plugs this at length). I can only say that I am tall and middle-aged and English by virtue of the fact that I am not short and young and Chinese! We live and have our being in a world of opposites, and when we wish to seek the Truth that lies between all of them we must first bring those opposites as near as possible. One way is by seeing the kernel of the opposite *in* its opposite, like the black and white symbols (I call them tadpoles) in the circle of the famous Chinese sign, where in the 'eye' of each is a dot of the opposite. No man is utterly good or evil, any more than he is utterly male or female. See the potentialities of each opposite in its other side; then bang their heads together, and in blinding light see darkness, in deafening noise hear the silence, in terrific all-out effort find complete passivity—then do them together! In meditation the mind must be held tense, one-pointed, bursting with the controlled energy of a tremendous will, and *at the same time*, relaxed, accepting, gentle, all but asleep. This is not the true Middle Way, a forced blend of the opposites, but it is some way towards the experience of a condition which is not this nor that but both/neither. Realise that *all* we say and do is wrong, being partial, and made up of half-truths of the opposites, and you will at least lift your eyes to the plane on which Truth alone can be found, above all pairs, in that state *before the pairing-off took place*. There is the middle of the Middle Way and only there.

And now I must seek to tread it in coping with a lady who is not sure if she would like to marry me, murder me, or both. And I have to be strong/tender, psychiatrical/human, patient/fierce, all at the same time, (while working out a talk for tonight *and* a speech for the defence tomorrow). And some people say life is dull!

Yours middling,

LETTER 80

Dear Clarence,

You are right that we are getting into very deep waters of thought as we approach, even in thought, that which must lie beyond it. As concepts tend to dissolve, and to be less sharp in outline, so the awareness or understanding, being more synthetic in the true sense of the term, is more embracing, and includes at once a dozen themes or truths, call them what you will. Or would it be better to say that as thought rises in quality it is less defined, i.e. confined, and more an increasing awareness of the indivisible Reality which we insult by attempting to chop it into pieces. We have been meditating together in Class on the 'Strength of no Desire' and 'Non-attachment'; also on the shift of centre, from self to something nearer No-Self; also on the Void or Sunyata which is full of everything, *every thing*, so full that it is No-thing. In such meditation it becomes more difficult to keep any subsequent talk in bounds, for there being no true 'distinction' between these themes, who are we to attempt to divide them? Perhaps the unifying theme of these is Dr Suzuki's 'self-identification', which I have been studying again in his *Mysticism, Christian and Buddhist* at p. 30. Buddhist philosophy, he says, is the philosophy of self-identity, which is to be distinguished from mere identity. For in the latter there are two things to be identified; in self-identity there is just one subject to be identified only, and this, he says, 'identifies itself by going out of itself', thus coming back to his graphic description to us of why God created the universe, and the Zen logic of No-logic in which A is A, and also not-A. But this self-identity he says 'is the logic of pure experience, or of "Emptiness", that is, Sunyata', and then, 'In this self-identity there are no contradictions whatever. Buddhists call this suchness'. In this brief paragraph is as much as the great man has said in several books! It is almost the ultimate synthesis of all his writing. And we've got to get there, to make it true, for us!

168

Thus concepts, thoughts of all kind, blend and blur; words fail as the noise of the unreal world fades slowly from the consciousness. Only in meditation, and afterwards, with a smile, a sigh or the holding up of a flower, is Reality attained and its awareness transmitted. Words are indeed useless at that level, but I am convinced that they must be used, in reading, talking and discussion, so long as they are useful at all. There is time, then, to abandon them. The rest is silence, and a finger pointing the Way.

Yours with a sigh,

LETTER 81

Dear Bungy,

So at last you can see straight? That's a nice bit of conceit! I am convinced that if we could really see straight, i.e. directly, see things as they are, we should be 'there'. To see *things* as they are is difficult enough, with their qualities of change or flux, with no 'soul', and somehow inseparable from suffering—yet in their suchness one with all other things; to see them not only one with other things but *as* those other things, as in 'the unimpeded interdiffusion of all particulars' (immortal phrase!) or Jijimuge. To see the nob-ness of the doornob and the appleness of the apple, and to see them as differently/one . . . You can do all this, can you? Clever girl, I wish I could. Yet people are *more* difficult, for *who* is my friend John, or Joan or what have you? One can see 'levels' in them as in oneself, of personality, deeper individuality, and something shining through, but to see them as they are? You're a clever girl. True, it is easier when one has learned at least in part to withdraw one's projections, so that one sees objectively and not through a cloud of liking, disliking, wanting, approval or disapproval and so on. Meanwhile we are all God/animals, and because we will not sufficiently admit the animal it is that much harder to find the God.

You talked before you went off about your reading. As you read quickly you can get through a good deal, but you may have reached the stage when too much intellectual stuff will cloud rather than clarify your mind. Now that you can see (more) straight I would suggest you choose those books which feed the intuition rather than the intellect, which 'make the bell ring'. Read with new eyes, seeing the experience which made the writer say what he did. Then chew and digest and absorb and *become* that wisdom. So, by being more you will do more and more rightly. I have long said that a sufficient library for a desert island could be 'put in a man's two pockets', and I used to say (in the twenties) that the lot could be bought for a £1 note. It is still not far from true. I would choose—if you want me to name a dozen—the *Voice of the Silence*, unless you are one of the curious few who, having heard vague reports of slanderous attacks on the translator, H. P. B., value the words the less; then the *Gita* and the *Tao Tê Ching*, each the distilled essence of the teaching of great minds; then, as they come to mind, the *Sutra of Hui-neng*, the *Diamond Sutra*, the fourth Gospel, *Eckhart*, *Huang-Po*, the *Dhammapada* and the *Heart-Sutra*. Of less 'Scriptural authority' I would add: Epictetus, Suzuki's *Introduction to Zen Buddhism* and (all but enough for me) the *Mahatma Letters to A. P. Sinnett* which, in preparing the third edition, I have read very carefully five times. How many lives will it be before we can speak from such a level of supernal wisdom? But in a way even these are not books to be 'read'. I remember when I first came across the *Voice of the Silence*, maybe in the edition to which the late Panchen Lama wrote the Foreword, and raving about it to an older student, I was crushed, with kind intent. 'You like it?' he said, 'I have only known it fourteen years but I agree that the first page—which is as far as I have got—is great indeed'.

Off you go and enjoy yourself. May I lend you a little light reading for the journey?

LETTER 82

Dear Mary,

So you are depressed with Mu, the eternal and uncompromising No. But why try a *koan* at all, and why this one, though it *is* most frequently given to beginners? I will make a suggestion, if you promise not to sneak about me to a Master. Try the opposite. Take a deep breath, stand upon a mountain-top and then, with all the strength of your lungs and will and the whole cosmic grandeur of you, yell, yell to the whole of all Creation—YES! Be blowed to the dialectical Nagarjuna with his eight Noes, and all the other Noes if there are any. Shout to the world that that which is utterly empty is utterly full. The Void is a Plenum—if nothing is true then all is true. Everything is, yes, *every thing*, or good or bad or large or small or splendid or very grubby indeed. It *is*, and it is part of all Creation, that ever-living, ever-growing, ever-becoming glory · which no-one created but which all enjoy. Yell YES until there is nothing left to yell, and what will you find? That 'God's in his heaven—all's right with the world'! Or, in the greater words of Thoreau, 'I know that the enterprise is worthy, I know that things work well. I have heard no bad news'.

The answer is Yes.

Yours ultimately affirmatively,

LETTER 83

From Notes to the Class
Before we part for the long vacation I have three things I would like to say. The first concerns myself. Some of you are leaning on me too much. Bear in mind always that I teach nothing, and the greatest Master would say the same. The Truth is within and no man can do more for another than to help him to find it. To some extent I hold up a mirror to your individual minds, as does a psychiatrist, or the parish priest. In it you see yourself. In return I see myself in you reflected, with all my insufficiencies. You are part of me. I love you, hate you, deplore you, am exasperated by you, as I love and hate those facets of myself I learned to behold objectively. These are selves and Selves but all one SELF. You know it, I know it; why, then, do we all behave as if we didn't? Use me, then; abuse me if you will. Love me or hate me or both at once, but don't lean on me, for you insult yourself thereby.

Why don't I give you koans for meditation? Because to 'solve' a koan means that you concentrate with every ounce of your will, over long periods of time, to achieve the impossible, to break through the barrier of thought to No-thought—with thought alone. You must exhaust the thought-machine as a horse that founders when it is galloped until it falls. Only in the moment of complete exhaustion comes the moment of complete surrender, and it is at *that* moment that one 'sees'. Such pressure deliberately worked up in a mind not quite balanced, with perhaps a hidden crack in it, is extremely dangerous. Only a Master, so called because he has been trained to teach, has any right to take that responsibility, to help work up that pressure and to sustain it to the end. In any event, I doubt if most of us are ready for that effort. Thirdly, and this is the 'new' reason, good or bad, as experience shall determine, I think the West must find a technique of its own, and until some genuine Teacher arrives in our midst, 'the latchet of whose shoes I am unworthy to unloose', I prefer to plough and sow with simple, safe, first principles. With these we are making great advances. Should we try for Everest before we are trained for the foothills? Yes, you say? Then go ahead; I am not stopping you.

And the third matter is the Goal of our endeavours. You are right, and I do not talk of it. I will tell you why. First, we should be concerned with causes and never with effects. If we are working on right lines the results will come. Secondly, what right have I to attempt to describe what I do not know? Could I tell you the subtle distinctions between Samadhi and Dhyana, between Dhyana and Prajna, between Prajna and Satori, and the nature of Nirvana? No, I could not, and if I could I should only be using words to describe what to you would remain as words. Don't then, let us waste time with definitions of the indefinable. There is work and enough in hand for years to come. About us lies the infinity of Here and Now, and ever to hand is This, the job in hand. And when experience comes it is well to remember the test by which to know if it is genuine. No experience is valid which still includes an I. I speak of Zen experience, and not of some state of trance in which to wallow in the comfort of serenity. I repeat, the man who describes an experience in which 'I' something or other, is lying. In Satori there is no I, for where there is I there is that which 'I' perceives, and that is two things (at least) and every spiritual experience has this in common, that it is the end, for that 'moment', of I. As one of you wrote to me, 'I stared at objects and tried to see them in "suchness". The result was a psychic "cross-eye" and puzzled frustration. So I gave it up and thought no more about it. Then one day I was idly looking at the young moon when suddenly I heard myself saying: "The moon *is* the moon".' Is this not worth all definitions and distinctions? Years ago in Japan, I spent a night in a Zen monastery, largely in meditation. As I left in the morning in a car with some of my young hosts we passed a cart. I noticed, as I had not 'seen' before, that the *wheels of a cart go round*. You

must forgive me. Since then I have not cared for the distinctions
in the aspects of the Supreme. It IS.

Peace be with you,

Part Three

EXPERIMENTS IN ZEN

CHAPTER VIII

EXPERIMENT IN ZEN

My article in the February issue on 'Zen Comes West'[1] has produced considerable comment, much of it in the answers to the third of three questions I put to members of the Zen Class. The purpose of the questions, to be answered not too briefly and in writing, was first, to make the members think clearly about their attitude to Zen and thus to learn much about themselves, and secondly to help me to place them for the coming session in the Beginners' Class, the Zen Class (closed for each Session) and the Circle, or inner group which meets at odd times just for meditation. Needless to say, a written paper was not the sole means of judgment but it is the only one of which anything may be published. Even the written papers were for my eye alone, but I have found the contents so profoundly interesting that, without breaking any confidence, I have thought it right to publish certain extracts and conclusions without delay. For this is the raw material of Western Zen, the unpolished and unedited expression of inner processes and direct experience which will help to decide the future of the Zen movement in Europe.

The three questions were:

1. Why have you chosen Zen Buddhism for your study, as distinct from any other school?
2. What do you mean by the Zen which you are seeking, and how fiercely are you seeking it? Add, if you wish, the results of your search so far.
3. I want your views on the suitability of Japanese Zen technique to Zen in the West. If not thought entirely suitable, I want your

[1] See page 126.

views on the best way of approaching, practising and teaching Zen in London in the absence of a qualified teacher.

The results were immensely different, extremely virile and often quite contradictory, exemplifying once again the two main types of the human mind. They cut across all differences of sex, age and education, and the profundity of opinion and experience was not commensurate with the time already spent on the study of Zen. The questions being interrelated the answers are often so blended that they overlap, but most of the twenty sets of answers so far received show that a spiritual yeast is working in the mind of the student, with results, pleasant or unpleasant, of illumination, frustration, utter despair, profound joy or merely a growing sense of the oneness of all things. But the yeast is working, and out of it will come, for better or worse, the school of English Zen. I say *English*, for other European races may take to it differently, even as we in the West may produce a form or vehicle of Zen very different from that of the Japanese. I have used italics to stress the point being made. All italics are mine.

1. *Why Zen Buddhism?*

Many students have travelled a long way before they arrived at Buddhism. Christian mysticism, Existentialism, Yoga, Theosophy, Spiritualism, New Thought, Psychology, Comparative Religion, even Catholicism, all had been tried and found wanting. The reasons were as varied as the substitutes rejected, but for many Buddhism was a relief from dogma, ritual and reliance on some Saviour. But why Zen Buddhism? Because the Theravada was not enough, being too limited. 'While Theravada is a cut and dried scientific and intellectual study of Buddhism, Zen is refreshingly revolutionary in its approach. All our upbringing with its conventions, convictions, rules, beliefs and dual thinking is only there to stimulate the ego. We must drop all this, and by means of our very conventions, rules, beliefs and dual thinking'. And another: 'Zen follows on as the next step after Theravada. After analysing all things until there is nothing left, it is essential to transmute that bleak nothingness into something alive; otherwise the intellectual barrenness of Theravada would lead to loss of balance'. And another: 'Any teaching that is developed, spoken and written down hardens and becomes more and more tainted. By the mere observance of such teaching one can never reach satori. Zen goes beyond the conceptual teaching of Buddhism to the very ground and meaning of the Buddha himself. The oneness of the Buddha was the life of his teaching, and Zen contacts this life and is one with its wholeness'.

Many stress this fact that Zen is whole, and all else partial. As a way it is the path to this unity; when achieved it is it. 'Zen incorporates life as a whole. Zen does not stand apart looking at it, or treating aspects of it. It does not moralise. It does not command, reward or punish. It invades and changes everyday life, giving each single moment its significance, but not disrupting the whole. It needs no intermediaries, it has the wonderfully cleansing effect of a violent thunderstorm. Its exclusion of formalism, its new, simple and direct method forces the mind to be at work continuously. Here seem to be rules made to be broken, methods presented only to be cast aside. Zen says: 'Don't accept, don't believe, don't submit. Break away from all you have ever known, tear it to pieces, then start from the beginning'. And again, 'My previous studies and experience have taught me that to meet the ever-changing NEW one has to meet it on its own terms with a fresh, *unconditioned vulnerability*'. This writer develops this theme later and his phrase opens up new vistas of comparison with new-found Western psychology.

But many reply with vehemence that they *didn't* choose Zen; Zen chose them, and they could not escape if they would, a perpetual echo of the theme of the Hound of Heaven. 'I did not choose Zen. A thirsty man doesn't choose water—he drinks it! Without any need of thinking there comes a response from within which knows —after its own fashion—beyond any need to justify itself to the intellect or to anyone else'. And again, 'Why should I seek that which I have? I can say with honesty that Zen pursues me all through the day and even when I neglect to be "mindful" my thoughts wander to the Class, to individuals on the same quest, to a Zen book, and so on'. And this writer speaks later of 'the energy which is ever beating at the final concept'. And a third, 'I didn't choose it; I found it and fell in head first, not understanding a word but having all my views turned upside down. It seemed easier like that, not more comprehensible, but somehow allowing for *the reasonableness of the absurd*'. How fascinating is that moment when reason is first bored with its own rationality!

179

Finally, many stress the importance of the teacher and of ample opportunity of access to him. As one writes, 'When Dr Suzuki came I understood directly with the heart as well as with the mind —the words were largely superfluous. It didn't matter that I was unable to remember much of his lecture afterwards. There had been a transmission of the Dharma to an infinitesimal degree and I was grateful for the experience'. Others develop this theme, that transmission is direct from a Master, but that a lesser teacher can stimulate the pupil to find Zen for himself—within.

What is Zen?

Most writers point out that it is impossible to answer this question, and that is true. 'The Tao that can be expressed is not the eternal Tao'. But having said this they deliver themselves of a wide variety of scintillating epigram, paradox, quotation and 'illumined confusion', if I may coin the phrase, which shows remarkable virility of experience. Many refer at once to its humour. 'Laughter is an essential ingredient in its method of work. Every other school of Buddhism is full of woe; yet Zen is founded on the same teachings and still comes up smiling'. It is direct. 'By Zen I mean the intuitive insight into real living as distinct from mere existence. If one could live each moment, then life would be bathed in flame of sunrise'. It must be used. 'Sometimes one feels as if Zen is an extension of oneself waiting to be used, if only one could catch up with it'. Another expands this. 'It is a means, a brush to paint with, a spade to till the earth. It must be used and not sought. If not used it can be a hindrance. We can *imagine* that we understand it, and produce a persistent and tenacious superiority. Apply it and use it, and the swollen ego deflates . . . I can't say I'm fiercely seeking it, but I'm trying to use it. I haven't got it, but I'm trying to use it . . .' This is pure Taoism and equally good Zen, for in use the user and the instrument are one. Another writes, 'I might write, "Zen is the experiencing of the moment without thought", but even as I write Zen has gone, together with the experience and the moment. Nevertheless in flowing with Zen as it flows I am *living life* as opposed to *thinking about living*, as we commonly do in the West'. 'Zen,' writes another, 'is a technique by which a man reaches unity by bringing it to life. It brings into unity the whole of life as lived from hour to hour. It leads to purposelessness, spontaneous, fearless living in which one is freed from the tension of "What ought I to do or to be"? It is a bird flying through space which has neither length, breadth, height or depth. It has nothing to teach . . .' Many speak of the Void, but one coins an excellent phrase. 'Zen is that which makes everything else seem empty'. The most common description is its completeness. 'Not in the sense of something coming to an end', one writes, 'but in the way that all things are balanced, the feeling that any situation is "just so", with no loose ends or ragged edges but complete in itself as a ball is complete'. But the final word is typical of its writer. 'The simple, honest, no-damn-nonsense of Zen carries its own conviction which brooks no dispute'.

Some deal separately with the results of Zen. 'A softening up of my own self-importance—a sense of inner space', writes one. 'In the performance of an ordinary task which ordinarily I might chafe at but which is now the only possible thing I could be doing, comes an awareness of its momentary "rightness".' Some results are surprising. 'Zen helps enormously in practical life, giving more common sense in handling mundane matters and people. Whilst Samsara and Nirvana are one they are completely distinct, and I see the meaning of "Render unto Caesar" . . .'

So much for Zen, from which we descend to the practical politics of

Zen for the West

Here there was so much diversity of view that it is difficult fairly to summarise. Generally speaking, there was a middle view about using Japanese technique. A late letter commenting on my 'Zen for the West' in the February issue speaks for many. 'I suggest that though Zen is not an art in itself it embraces the greatest art of all, the art of living. As in every art the student must learn techniques and disciplines; he must find a form to canalise his inspiration, and unless he is a genius, he must at first *borrow* forms until he can devise his own. Thus the musician will listen to music of other times and places, and will begin by writing music in the manner of the masters. The writer will read all he can, and his first attempts will be modelled on work that has stood the test of time; only when he has mastered certain techniques and learned the rules, can he afford to break those rules and formulate his own. So with Zen; here we have no pattern but that set by the East, and we must learn it and practice it with diligence, until such time as a creative artist appears in this art so strange to us, and formulates a technique more akin to our way of life. It cannot be forced—if Zen is *here*, as I believe, the art-form will arise naturally in the fullness of time. Be patient, my masters'.

On the use of the koan there is much debate. Some say it is the life of Rinzai Zen; others that it is folly to attempt it in the absence of a Master. One points out that daily life is full of koans and we have to solve them anyway. All agree on the need for more and more meditation, for whatever the methods used each in the end must 'go it alone'. But several agree that this is a dangerous business. 'Passionate conflicts, desperate confusions and the like are inevitable. It is here that the authority and accessibility of the teacher are vital. He can help the student to understand that these things are mind-made and can be destroyed by the mind which made them'. Several stress that, 'we are brought up in a climate of thought so different from that of the East that we are totally unprepared for its anarchism unless we have first made acquaintance with the Dharma proper'. No student, thinks this writer, 'should be accepted in a Zen class unless he has belonged to the Society for at least a year, attending other lectures or meetings, or can *prove* that he has acquired a good grounding in Buddhism. He must learn discrimination in the Buddhist sense before he is told to reject it. In the West we live amid discriminations, and the ability to make a wise choice must be developed before the student can be safely told that there is no problem, no right and wrong, and that spontaneity is all. Shock tactics are splendid so long as the audience have built up some orthodox strength beforehand . . .' But the process is individual, and many agree that for it we need more silence, more week-end retreats, with less book-learning and more 'mindfulness'.

We must avoid, say many, the stereotyped formula, of words or action, and be perpetually new. 'The freshness of any discovery, phrase or word becomes stale with repetition, but if new words, new phraseology is demanded, deeper implications and discovery follow as the thing is viewed anew'. But we must be intellectual before we can pass beyond the intellect; we must learn to think before we achieve No-thought.

Whether we use the fierceness of Rinzai Zen or the passivity of Soto Zen, which no doubt equally leads to the Goal, is a matter of opinion in which the writers inevitably divide out into the complementary types of mind. One typical of others, writes, 'We don't want additional knowledge—we want to "undress" until there is nothing left but the Buddha-nature. And this for me can only be achieved by the shock-treatment of Zen—the direct approach'. Others entirely disagree. 'We come to realise that the only thing to do is let go, to give up'. We need patience, they say, not violence. The answer, of course, is a middle way, and perhaps one of our wisest members may have the last word. 'It would be better for Zen in the West to work out its own technique. This it appears to be doing . . .'

Such are a few spoonfuls from the cauldron of the Zen Class of the Society. It is bubbling mightily. There will be scum to remove, steam to let off, but this is the spirit moving, in its own time and in its own way. No short cuts are attempted, no tricks allowed. Whether we reach any Goal is beside the point. We are past such folly as seeking one. But at least, while awaiting further assistance, advice or rebuke, we are fiercely, mightily, Zennishly alive.

CHAPTER IX

FURTHER EXPERIMENT IN ZEN

In 'Experiment in Zen', which appeared in the May issue, I said that the cauldron of the Zen Class of the Society was bubbling mightily. It has now bubbled over into a further experiment, in the group consideration of individual problems, with no apologies to similar experiments in the field of psychology. Meanwhile, as the previous article only reported about half the answers to the first question paper, and as the remainder were if anything of a higher standard still, I have asked the Editor to let me have space for further comment. The keynote is still the intense virility of personal experience, with the authority of scriptures and well-worn phrases, and all 'isms, even Buddh-ism, left behind. I warned the class of the old and occult law by which any deliberate, planned and sustained effort to take the 'shadow' self in hand and to expand consciousness ahead of the average of one's friends and associates, produces its own fresh crop of *dukkha* (suffering), on the mental, emotional and even physical planes. And the troubles came, so thick and fast that I was glad that the sufferers were duly warned. There is indeed a need, as one writer puts it, 'to grade the Class and Circle and Group in respect of the teaching given and the exercises demanded with some kind of appraisal of psychological maturity'. But the suffering will be felt, whatever the grade, until the end of self. As the same writer elsewhere says, 'Only by dying to myself in the moment, to words, thought, and even to the desire to die, can Zen be revealed. Only then is the actor and the action one, and the problem and the solution the same'. For the material of the Zen search is life itself. The secret lies 'in accepting life as it presents itself'. Again, 'the task of being alive is to live. To contemplate the futility of it all, and the suffering of it all, thus severing oneself from life, seems to me still a form of escape'. The same happy mind goes further, 'Zen is my way, and I shall go it because I cannot go any other. Besides, I like it. I do not have a goal to which to strive, but simply enjoy walking . . . the movement of the walking on is joy'. And as another points out, and psychologists would heartily agree, the walk is with the whole man. 'Because man strives to be whole he is not,' and we cannot leave the part of ourselves we loathe and despise at the foot of the hill while the 'better Self' climbs to the top. 'When illumination comes it illumines all of us', and, as another says, 'the goal and the way cannot be different; one finds the way by treading it, one's spiritual forces by using them, and without humility and poverty one gets nowhere at all.' 'Zen,' says another, 'is in the living of the moment; it is not to be found anywhere, but comes from an unfolding centre'. Or, as yet another writes, 'the experience of Zen is within this life; Zen is here, not a state to be sought outside life. Religious activity is activity on the plane of daily life', which another caps magnificently with, 'I regard Zen as the religion to abolish all religion. The word religion means a rebinding . . . but Zen, at the supreme moment, swallows itself'.

As for Zen in the West, these later writers emphasise the need of understanding Zen as it is before seeking to reclothe it; 'else we are in danger of confusing the clothes with Zen, the finger with the moon'. As a woman writer shrewdly points out, we have been supplied with Zen literature for years and yet are still saying 'Give us Zen'. 'We must beware of adding another technique to our collection, and choose between the technique and Zen, which laughs at all systems and teaching.' Most, however, agree that for a time we must have a qualified *roshi* to help us, though in the end we must produce our own. Meanwhile, Zen scriptures will help, backed by an indomitable will which in the end will create and use the necessary means.

Such was the position at Easter. From then until June, the Society was favoured with the successive presence of three men well-known in the world of Zen. Dr Hisamatsu, a lay *roshi* and expert on Japanese art, though hampered by the need of translation in what he said, showed us what a *roshi* can be. Alan Watts, now a well-known writer and speaker in Zen Buddhism, showed us the thoughts of one of the leading minds in Western Zen; then came Dr Suzuki himself, a man who, having attained his own Zen enlightenment, has spent just sixty years offering it to the West. Yet, as one student wrote, 'the Masters can but give us encouragement, tell us when we are getting warm, and confirm our arrival. No Master has ever claimed more than this'. Dr Suzuki, apparently impressed with the strenuous efforts of the Class to find Zen and to accept no substitutes, has promised to persuade one or more Japanese but English-speaking *roshis* to spend substantial time in Europe in the near future. Meanwhile I gave the members a new set of questions.

1. How does Zen, or your search for Zen, affect your daily life— your thinking, feeling, reactions, values, motives, acts?
2. How in meditation do you attempt to pass the pairs of opposites which are inherent in all thought, and so achieve direct experience of non-duality?
3. How do you understand the passive acceptance of all conditions and events, and how do you collate this with the effort or energy which it seems necessary to use in order to achieve any progress or 'experience'?

The answers were not always given seriatim as in an examination paper, and many members regarded all three as nine-pins to be knocked flat with tremendous gusto. One must be quoted at length, for it was long before I picked myself up off the floor. 'If the search for Zen affects one's outlook vastly, it probably means that one was not really of a suitable make-up for this particular path. A tree does not search for its fruits, it grows them. So should one's pursuit of Zen be the result of one's attitude to life, and not be regarded as a new line to follow. It is useless for a pear tree to desire apples. Thus I do not use Zen practices to reform myself but to express myself'. And that's that.

Others, less fiercely direct, talk of the 'horrible little self' which must be faced, admitted to exist, and included in the total 'Self' which is advancing. For them 'Zen creates a background against which thoughts, feelings and personal troubles are seen as forms of limitation'. Or to use another analogy, 'Everything seems like parts of one big picture, each part being as important, or not important, as each other'. But the great discovery of many members is the direct approach to things as they are. 'Whatever the matter to be done, it is approached on its own level, with eager friendliness accepted in its own right and carried through with the fullest attention and devotion one can give. One rises to the situation, assimilates it, lives in it, and the action gets accomplished so.' When youth is thus on the right lines what will its owner not accomplish in age? 'We must learn to live in the present,' says another, 'but there must be "more looking".' 'I live more intensely.' writes another, 'while I think and therefore worry less'. And the 'looking' or objective examination of all things and events may be and should be carried out, not with a weary eye on *dukkha* (suffering), but with joie de vivre, the 'spontaneous knowledge of a dynamic livingness'. 'How absurd it is to drag the past into the present, so beautifully alive'. 'My search for Zen has chiefly brought me joy,' writes another, and this is sharply distinguished from the pleasures of the senses. 'Other people are taken more for what they are than what I want them to be,' writes one who has not heard of Jungian 'withdrawal of projections' but is doing it. And this withdrawal produces a greater independence of external factors, a greater detachment from events, a loosening of ties, 'detachment as distinct from indifference'. 'I have at long last really seen the point of depending only on oneself—the wonderful release in abandoning all hope.' Applying the same discovery another says, 'As I see it, the Zen Buddhist observes the code of conventional morality not because he considers it to have any intrinsic value but because the reasons which might impel the ordinary person to break it do not operate in his case', which is to many of us an utterly new idea.

Several have found their way to the mighty saying, 'All that happens happens right', one member by loosening the hold of the dichotomy of like and dislike, which is coupled, the writer finds, with an increasing respect for other people, 'unaffected by the fact that their acts, emotions and ideas may be at complete variance with one's own. Life is truly one.' For this member, tragedy has lost its value—'for what can go wrong?' Just 'allow things to happen. Zen says get out of the way, and the effort one has to make is just to get out of the way'. With all this new awareness comes a new understanding of compassion, as the necessary fruits of the oneness of life. One writes of 'the suffering of others about which I can do nothing that causes me intense anguish of spirit'. Another could help her, with his analysis of all sense of suffering into concepts which can with effort be discarded. Regret for the past and anxiety about the future are alike thought-forms, ensouled with imagination. But this is itself of the intellect and the heart still suffers, and must suffer until of each burning human tear it may be said 'thyself hast wiped it from the sufferer's eye'. Only the mind in Prajna can cease from such reaction, and the Bodhisattva heart does not choose to do so.

For asking question 2, I was rebuked by the same writer who dealt so pungently with question 1. 'I do not regard the pairs of opposites as parallel lines which can never meet. I realise that in passing beyond them I bring them with me in another form. Were I to reject the opposites I should simply create a new pair, duality versus non-duality. So to achieve the experience of non-duality I must cease to concern myself with it as such, because it is impossible to "regard" anything in a non-dualistic manner. Therefore I attempt to lose all sense of "regarding".' With some writers I should be tempted to consider this slick intellectuality. Here, it is, I think, genuine experience. Many others speak of the watching, or regarding or steady looking at things, and this is common ground to many schools of Buddhism. One describes it as in the field of psychology. 'I have become aware of this search (for Zen) as if it were a dance between the inner and outer life. One just sits and watches, and magic things stir in the dark waters preparatory to rising to the surface. What forms they will take I do not know, but they live and have strong powers of movement and vitality.' This increasingly objective attitude to mental happenings is all to the good, for it develops the power to withdraw projections, on which Jung lays so much stress, and restores the integrity of the 'whole man' who must use the 'one-moment' of timelessness for every act. Some tackle the opposites from the top, that is, from the concept of that in which they are subsumed and merged in one (while remaining two). 'I start with an attempt to drop "self", and then try to concentrate on the theme from the top of the triangle. Then other "thoughts" come through, as though released, but they are not "thoughts".' But as another points out, the experience of 'non-duality has nothing to do with thinking, and we must simply let the truth of this operate'. It operates 'by relieving one of a host of concepts. We are free to pay attention to the task in front of us. Walking is walking and eating is eating . . .' (Thus are famous Zen phrases reborn in Western minds in the crucible of experience).

I will close this section by quoting an experience which calls for no comment. 'I started on the opposites without knowing it by following the instructions in *The Cloud of Unknowing*. I said one short word, God, and repeated it until my mind was saying it in rhythm with my breathing, 23 hours a day, non-stop. This created an acute tension, and I could not distinguish between God and the Devil. This produced an awful despair. I felt I was too evil to recognise goodness . . . Still the Hound pursued, and the tension grew. Then I came home—to Zen. I meditated on the opposites. As any thought came to me I pushed it into the unconscious and left the whole lot to simmer. Then one day it all boiled over and took possession of me. I went round with a certainty that I was going mad, muttering to myself "Nirvana and Samsara, they are one". Then one afternoon in Kensington Gardens I gave up. I sat looking at the flowers, completely exhausted. Gradually I was aware of an all pervading calm, pouring in. At last I was at peace, and the Hound no longer pursued me. I know that I know, but what I know I do not know'.

About passivity in action or effort-less energy the battle raged merrily. Most were agreed on the necessity of cultivating acceptance, of circumstances outside and also within the mind. Many invoked the law of karma. 'I never have willingly lain down under adversity, but I have learned the wisdom of inner acceptance through my faith in the law of Karma. My (very Western) instinct is to take immediate action, but I sometimes find acceptance itself to be a form of action.' And another: 'the passive acceptance of all conditions and events is absolutely necessary for they are our karmic balance carried forward from our previous births'. Some find the effort to accept considerable. 'Sustained effort is needed to break through the layers with which we have surrounded Reality, and this energy is in no way affected by acceptance of present conditions.' Another puts this negatively. 'Passivity in my case means throwing off compulsions and inhibitions,' but the throwing off is a form of effort. Effort is truly necessary, and we must accept, as one puts it, the necessity of effort! Perhaps acceptance comes first. 'If I wish to drop a particular habit I must just drop it; it is useless to get involved with self-reproaches, resolutions and moralising, a method which resembles one's attempt to get rid of a sticky piece of paper . . . ' So the writers get closer and closer to the resolution of the tension. One sees the pair as pull and push. 'The Absolute pulls the relative particle as a magnet an iron filing; the filing pushes to reach the Absolute.' Another gets nearer still. 'I don't see the problem here. You see a problem only if you think energy can't operate without a conscious object to strive towards. But attachment only dissipates energy . . .' (I think of Suzuki's 'The strength of no desire'.) Yet another is perhaps nearer still. 'Passive acceptance is only a fact when I stand face to face with a fact accepting it for what it is, without excusing it or trying to change it. It is what it is—in that point-instant of the moment . . . The clarity of perception which enables one to face a fact or situation with all one's attention manifests one's dynamism, effort or energy, and one's action is but the unimpeded continuity with which the situation is dealt with . . .'

These are but sayings and thoughts collected from some 30 papers averaging 300 words. Some are finding the pace too hot for them; they are resting and may renew the battle later. But others, so far from being pursued by the Hound of Heaven are in full cry after the Hound and yelping with happy excitement. What a Master would think of it all I know not, but I think he would smile, and the smile would be full of Zen.

CHAPTER X

THIRD EXPERIMENT IN ZEN

Nature proceeds by jumps and pauses, seldom by that 'steady progress' beloved by Chairmen of City Companies, and the answers to the third set of questions were in the main uninspired. The first two questions were:—

I. What is the relation between your present inner self-development and the awakening of Bodhi-citta, compassion for all forms of life and their suffering?

II. 'Usual life is very Tao (or Zen)'. Interpreted superficially this is a dangerous half-truth; deeply understood it might become the foundation of Western Zen. What is your understanding?

The third question, the relation between divers well-known and much quoted sayings, was not, perhaps, happily conceived for arousing the intuition and will here be ignored.

A fourth set of questions covered the ground of the above two but went deeper. The results were fascinating, and produced the finest fire-works display of intuitive flashes yet achieved. The questions were:—

1. Karma has been called the law of harmony, and breaches of the law produce effects on the breaker. Compassion has been called 'the Law of Laws, eternal Harmony'. Can you 'see' that Karma and Compassion are truly aspects of one law of Harmony? If so, show me that you 'see'.

2. 'Every-day mind is Zen'. 'Usual life is very Tao'. 'It's here, in the dust-bin'. All true, but how true to you? Show me.

3. 'Be humble and remain entire'. This is a quotation in the Tao Tê Ching, which shows it is old indeed, perhaps one of the oldest truths in the hearts of men. How true is it to you?

The Class has now reached the stage when individual development, and the great variety of roads along which it is achieved,
produce a complexity of 'level', 'field' and method of approach
which, in a body of thirty London citizens may well be an epitome
of the city, of the country and, possibly, of the Western mind.
Types have become clear-cut, the natural mystic, the intuitive-
intellectual, the philosophic-ritualist, the Taoist gardener, the
extraverted, self-analysing psychologist and a dozen more, most of
them remarkably tolerant, in a deep sense, of each others' profoundly different line of approach to the same Reality. But in each
member the distinctions between hit and miss, often seen by the
writer, are equally apparent. One writes 1200 words on the first
question, producing a first-class article on the subject, but heavily
intellectual, and then in a dozen lines for question 2 hits, as it were,
the ceiling with intuitive awareness. The speed of reaction is so
different as to be embarrassing. Some of the best Answers come
through the post in a few days; others complain at the end of two
months that they are still 'simmering' and the answer has not yet
'come through'. But all have a deeper sense of integration, with
life, with circumstance, with each other and all that lives. One,
for example, after a class at which we had discussed the 'closing
of the gap' between Nirvana and Samsara, wrote a sudden post-
card in the middle of the morning's household chores: 'What
waste of time—sweating away to close the gap that isn't there!
Our distress comes from trying to pull the One apart and make it
two, and it won't budge. No wonder we get a bit tired!'

It will be convenient to consider together No. 1 of the third set
of questions on compassion, and No. 1 of the fourth set on compassion, harmony and karma.

These concepts, and the deep religious and spiritual realities
they symbolise, were found so interlinked that it was evidence
of an incipient and growing awareness of their basic unity. Most
took as their basic concept, Harmony. 'The universe is one and
indivisible. Hence the law of Harmony governs it. Everybody and
everything influences every other thing and every other body, and
is in turn influenced by them. A polar bear coughs at the North
Pole and the sands of the Sahara stir. There is no separate self.
Cosmic energy is not divided into individual persons. Compassion
is the outcome of this knowledge . . .' And again, 'Life is stark

real, vitally alive and so closely interwoven that no distinction
is possible. All is an inside-outside relationship, all equally part
of my 'set-up' and in daily life one sets off every moment a new
chain-reaction. It is breath-taking. I watch and react and become
and change and flow . . . inside-outside, where is the border?'
From this unceasing 'changing, merging, altering, being born and
dying, each ephemeral object's karma is its potential, its innermost
becoming manifest in space-time. Thus myriads of potentials of
karma stream out from one in all directions to embrace the whole
universe. Viewing one man's life, his Karma gives it homogeneity,
forms it into a living whole so that his past lives on with him.'

Another takes it up. 'The deepening understanding of the oneness
of life produces an equally growing compassion for all forms of life.
Then the stone is my brother . . . But I must have experienced it
myself. Only then is my compassion a reflex action at one with life,
and has the warmth of it, and the 'whole-making' effect. If it is self-
motivated, even with the best motives, it causes results, hence
Karma.' Here enters self. 'It is our own sick-mindedness that
prevents us having a natural, spontaneous compassion for other
people.' And again, 'We become aware of Karmic laws only when
we stop becoming objective in our attitude to life. Only a sense of
'I' can interfere with Harmony, for Harmony is undivided and it is
the sense of 'I' which divides . . . The awareness of Karma shows
we are off-balance, as the Law is only felt in dualism. We are
unaware of Compassion; when we are aware of it it is not compassion.' To see dually, several conclude, is due to the Karma
created by disturbance of the Harmony which only Compassion,
spontaneously arising, can restore. 'When we are out of step with
the oneness, Karma is required to restore the balance.'

But we must be aware of the break, the disturbance, before we
can cure it; else we are merely pushed about by the Law. 'To rise
one must start at the bottom. There must be a known break before
a making whole.' 'The laws of Karma are our teachers if we can
recognize Compassion at work beneath them.' 'Compassion'
writes another, 'is the constant, conscious desire to bless anyone
anywhere, as they touch our consciousness. In this I fulfil my own
law of Harmony, or pay the price for not so doing.'

Another writes, 'I see both Karma and Compassion as the 'skilful means' of one law of Harmony, two brooms both sweeping

the path that leads to Harmony.' But here comes a gentle reproof for talking about 'laws', lest we imagine a law-giver. 'It is not that Karma exists and we fit into it, but Karma is the word we use to describe our actions and reactions.' That is well said. Several imported suffering as the factor common to these concepts. 'Only the acceptance of one's own suffering leads to a willingness to share in the suffering of others', writes one, and another may mean the same thing when he asks that we spare a little time to be sorry for ourselves. For it is the self that causes all the trouble. Adds another, 'What a paradox it is that to drop the self one must first experience it, live with it, examine it; these feelings of pride, fear and the like dissolve not by being rejected but by being lived with.' Thus is Karuna born. It cannot be aroused deliberately though we can and should act 'as if', by living 'as if' the flame were already awake. But because a 'Compassion can only manifest itself unselfconsciously, a compassionate man would be in a sense unaware that it had arisen in him.' Hence the truly compassionate act is spontaneous, without thought before or recollection afterwards. For as another wrote, 'After years of wringing my heart with sympathy for others' suffering I realise that this is no true compassion but a form of self-indulgence.' The ideal, thinks another, is to act naturally, natural to the mind that has ceased to see people as separate entities and knows them as now One.

So 'the debate continues'—about a general concept of the Universe as in Harmony, with self-ful actions breaking that Harmony, to the debit of the one who broke it. Compassion is seen as the healing force which makes *one* where the disturbance of the equilibrium and oneness had made two, the healing or 'whole-ing' power to offset the destructive force of our folly.

2. From struggling in the coils of these tremendous principles the Class turned to the more extravert conception of 'usual life' or 'everyday mind' as 'Tao' or 'Zen'. The danger referred to in the original question is very real. It is far too easy to assume that 'ordinary life' lived in the full measure of habitual fatuity will in some way one day produce enlightenment. This was far from the purpose of the creator of the original phrase. In the 19th item in the *Mumonkwan*[1] we read, 'Nansen was asked by Jyoshu, "What is Tao?" Nansen answered, "Ordinary mind is Tao". "Should we try

[1] See *Zen for the West*, Ogata. Rider & Co., p. 108.

to get it?" asked Jyoshu. "As soon as you try you miss it", was the master's reply.' The point, as most writers discovered, is in Suzuki's words, 'There is nothing infinite apart from finite things', and as a member put it, 'This and here and now is the field of experience. If we run to the farthest ends of the world we cannot escape from ordinary life. Where else can we go for Enlightenment?' Therefore, 'relax into life as it comes', says one, 'not living for the special occasions and disregarding what goes between. Let daily life just be; do every little thing whole-heartedly and relinquish it without regret when done.' As to what mind to use, 'what other mind have I but my everyday mind?' asks one. 'Only a hypocrite has a Sunday mind. Zen is whole, all, everything, in what one finds as in what one rejects of pain, humility and daily work.' All this is obvious, writes another, 'so obvious that how can I *show* you my understanding? Can one describe the taste of water?' What is needed, many agree, is 'an unusual way of living usual life.' To live in the moment is the secret, find several. 'But living in the now is an impossibility without giving up the desire for past and future, and a willingness to accept the now whether nice or nasty.' The trouble as ever is the self. 'It simply cannot bear to be left out of anything.' But need it be? 'Life in the Tao-way is pure action within the "moment". No thinking, no speculating before, during or after the act. The act fills up the whole of the moment . . . (What a phrase! Is this an echo of Kipling's "If you can fill the unforgiving minute with sixty seconds' worth of distance run . . .?). If we could live thus all the time we should be enlightened.' The violent effort to see in the ash-tray the whole universe is waste of time. It is there, but so long as there is a seer and a seen, there are two things, and the truly 'usual' life is lived in non-duality. For Zen is freedom, and only the free man, made free by Prajna, can live the purposeless life of Zen which, seeing no distinctions, or seeing them as the mind-born children of illusion, is equally content with a dust-bin or a symphony, sewing on a button or trying on a crown. 'All this implies struggle, but this struggle is quite useless and leads no-where. Yet without it the next stage would never happen. This is when the struggle is given up, and until this happens there can be no enlightenment.' But Zen, says another, 'releases the energy once wasted in dealing with the confusion of the relative world. Am I on the right path? Am I doing the right thing? Zen is confident and free from anxiety.' 'It is when we "drop it" that we *know* . . . Zen is unknowable, indescribable, but it works.' Thus the *Tao Tê Ching* has the last word. 'When one looks at it one cannot see it. When one listens to it one cannot hear it. But when one uses it it is inexhaustible.' Applying this, a new member preferred to express herself in verse:

> As I make my every day,
> I look upon people, places, things,
> Label them good or bad, high or low,
> Mine and thine.
> And thus divided, they confuse me.
>
> But when as an arrow
> Loosed by It
> I touch the Centreless Centre,
> Where to put a dustbin—
> Or yet a diamond—
> Or even me?
>
> After that, in usual life,
> When a mudbank or a star I see,
> I smile,
> And let it be.

3. 'Be humble and you will remain entire.' I have long been fascinated by the fact that this phrase was thought so great that it is actually quoted in the *Tao Tê Ching*, itself one of the greatest Scriptures in the world. Many members in my view missed the grandeur entirely, and reduced it to a trite admonition against personal conceit. Some even objected to the word humility as smacking of humiliation. The individual *must* assert himself at times, else he remains one of the herd—and so on. A few got near to the heart of the tremendous statement by grasping the word 'remain', and some of these appreciated that 'it is a state of mind directly conditioned by the heart.' Or, as another put it, 'This is the heart of the matter but it must not be separated from the head, for in Zen there cannot be two ways. The pilgrims walk on this or other paths, yet there is only one pilgrim and he must become the

Path to tread it.' But we must *remain* entire, 'and not cut off the bit of us we don't like. We must accept our Wholeness.' As another wrote, 'I must step down to step up,' which reminds me of my favourite saying of a pupil long ago, 'Before we can become extra-ordinary we must learn to become extra ordinary!' The facet of acceptance was much to the fore. 'To live life humbly is not to make demands of it, not to reproach it, to ask no more than the present moment brings.' We must be content to be nothing as such. 'You are the froth and the foam on the waves of the sea. Let the froth dissolve into the wave, and make the relaxing, expanding, interior gesture towards the freedom of the total sea'. 'No man', wrote another, 'is greater than his power to humble himself.' The secret is to remain in this entirety. Yet another is, I think, nearer the mark still. 'The clue is in the word remain. Entirety does not come after being humble. 'The entirety of being humble is the absence of concern over an "I" .' But self has many meanings. As another put it, 'To be humble is to remain with oneself. Not to journey outwards in search of treasure, but to search in one's own cup-board for the widow's mite. Humility knows no fear; for loss and gain are of no account to it. The humble man neither gives nor takes hostages in a war with fortune; he remains simple and unconfused. One cannot decide to be humble. Humility is a by-product of Self-knowledge.'

To the answers to this question I would add one word of my own. In meditation I have begun the other end, with the word entire. Here is the primordial Absolute, one's 'original Face before one was born'. This should never be lost, for it is in the littlest act of the daily round, and never ceases to be. To assert self is to break this harmony, unity, wholeness. Karma steps in to regulate the return to Harmony, to persuade one of the wisdom of remaining entire. This wisdom we call humbleness, non-self-assertion. By it we *remain—entire*.

So much for a brief review of the answers to these two sets of questions, in which I trust that I have not lost the light of intuition which made so many of them so worth while. At least it is a record of experience, and I will end with the words of one of the students on this theme. 'From birth to death all one has is one's experience. This goes on whether one names it or not. Experience is an in-dividual matter, and can only be known as it becomes conscious of its flow, for to name an experience is to give to a passing flow the semblance of fixity. But the world seen as a conglomeration of fixed entities is an illusion, and the attempt to hang onto the flow is where suffering arises. Emptiness being form and form being emptiness, life arises out of the void at each "moment", or between each two "moments", and each of these gaps is the Void of eternity. To this supreme experience I have not yet come, but from this side of that experience I can hear it in a half-comprehending silence.' It is in the silence that we shall know.

CHAPTER XI

SURVEY AND PROPHECY

The theme and scope of this brief work were outlined in the Preface. Now the reader has all the material available to form a just opinion on this situation, in which a great teaching of the East awaits a Western mode of expression.

SURVEY

At least the following facts have emerged. 1. That Zen Buddhism, in its fifteen hundred years of history, has become a strongly woven tradition, of a master or Roshi who has gained his enlightenment and been taught to help others towards the same experience; of a technique of 'direct transmission' which only when the initial impulse had a little waned produced the famous *koan* and *mondo* system for leading beyond thinking to No-thought; and of a goal, called *satori*, which is a timeless, self-less 'moment' of enlightenment, of Non-duality. This tradition created and still uses its special technical terms and almost its own language. It uses but few scriptures but these are so well known that the subtlest allusion to a passage in them is at once picked up. Within this tradition and by this technique of 'wordless transmission' many have achieved their enlightenment, but 'many' must be considered in the framework of fifteen centuries wherein at any one time there may have been a million men who strove for this enlightenment. And of those who achieved the 'great experience' or achieved it more than a few times in a strenuous life of spiritual endeavour, how many existed at any one time—or today?

2. The second fact is that Zen Buddhism was brought to the

West by Daisetz Teitaro Suzuki. Still active in his ninetieth year, this great mind, perhaps the greatest living in the field of religious experience, achieved his enlightenment in 1896, and has spent the rest of his long and active life in making known to the West the doctrines, the principles and the active way of Zen. With two exceptions, every writer on Zen whose works I know has admitted his debt to Dr Suzuki, and if ever one man gave a great tradition to the other hemisphere this is he. Alan Watts, myself, Benoit, Linssen and 'Wei-wu-wei' all drew from him the main source of our knowledge, such as it is, and the possibility of our experience whatever that may have been. These are facts. But though Dr Suzuki has promised to find some Japanese Roshi to live with us in Europe and teach the few found worthy the way to Zen experience, it will be hard indeed to find such a master, with a good knowledge of English and Western ways, willing to come and to stay, and able to find employment for his time in a community where the students will for the most part have but a small part of their lives to give to him.

Yet the West is interested, deeply interested, not only in the history, scriptures and tradition of Zen Buddhism but in the search for Zen. Why? That is a question easier to ask than to answer, but it must be to fill some need. The gap left in the minds and hearts of those who no longer find sufficient nourishment in the Church in which they were born is not being filled with the substitutes of science and psychology, or whatever be the chosen god to replace the God discarded. Yet, and here is irony, these new gods are changing in their form and message so profoundly and so rapidly that day by day they are moving nearer to the house of Zen. The mind of psychology is fast expanding, moving towards Mind; the very matter which is the food of science daily shrinks into mere force or motion, while the paraphernalia of social science, cradled in politics, is only the practice of the principles long taught by every mystic and in every hall of Zen, that life is one, that men are brothers, and that in the end the last blade of grass will enter into Buddhahood.

This interest in Zen, which is so friendly to the gods of Western thought, of yesterday, today or tomorrow, for it lives in all of them, is shown in a hundred ways; by the sale of books on the subject, by talk over the table of thinking minds, in jokes and poems and even in advertisements, in the number of those who ask for help to pursue their studies to the end. The interest is less obvious on the Continent, too obvious in the U.S.A. where it has already de-generated, as was to be expected, into a foolish and rootless cult. But in a recent article in *The Young East*, Spring, 1959, Professor van Meter Ames describes in remarkable detail comparisons between the Zen attitude to facts and circumstance and that of American daily life. He seeks to find Christian terms for Zen experience, and why not? Dr Suzuki is immensely impressed with Eckhart, and quotes long passages to support and exemplify his own teaching. And the car-driver, asks Dr Ames, tense yet relaxed, with a wide field of vision yet with full attention here or there as required, expecting the unexpected and ever at one with the total situation, including his own body and his car, is this a worse illustration for the man of Zen than that of the fencer or the man of Judo waiting for the timeless 'moment' in which to attack? But if this is a pioneer article on the subject there will soon be more. For the Western mind is very much alive, and looking for new forms of the one life which, at spiritual or material level, has no one home.

The problem, then, is clear. How to supply and satisfy this interest with effective leadership, advice and training towards the seen but unexperienced end? There seem to be four possible answers.

1. Some Westerners have visited Japan and studied there, after learning Japanese, with Japanese Roshis. More could do this, a few with success, but not many more at a time, and certainly not hundreds.

2. Japanese Roshis could learn English, study Western modes of life and thought, and come to the West to teach those ready to learn, and to pay the price for learning. So far we have heard of few who would qualify, and of none willing to give up years to such a task. Only those still reasonably young would be suitable, with ways of thought still supple, and prepared to spend a large part of the day in some other employment.

3. Or one or more Englishmen could train so far in Japan that not only would they achieve their enlightenment, but be further taught how to teach, and thus become Roshis which, as shown, is a high degree indeed. There is none yet that we know

who is even in training for such a course, which must, in the nature of things be a matter of long years.

4. What else? We are none of us willing to stand still for five or ten or fifteen years; certainly no one who knows of the Zen command, 'Walk On!'. Zen Buddhism is a Japanese form or set of clothing for a spiritual experience which is not Japanese but human. In the human mind is a spring of creative life which creates the right form for itself through the ages, and in different parts of the world. We say that the Zen experience is the same wherever found, and that given the life-force urgent to burst its fetters they will break. True, we shall miss the bull's eye a thousand times for every shot we land on the target, and well we know that 'half an inch and it is worlds apart.' But is that a reason for not training the muscles which will in time draw back the bow to loose the arrow to hit the target of satori?

The difficulties ahead are enormous, but what is large or small to the man of Zen? In Japan the raw material for Zen training is the young male, backed with a thousand years of the same tradition, having never learnt to vaunt his intellect beyond his intuition, and giving his whole time, twenty-four hours a day, to his *koan* or whatever the task in hand may be. In London we have a class of men and women, of all types and ages, of different race and widely different backgrounds. The heavy intellectual, the born mystic, the intuitive-emotional, the practical Martha, the devoted Mary; even the neurotic genius, we have them all and more. And many are beginning the journey with the set habits of middle-age. All these meet, not fresh at dawn, but after a long day's work, a substantial journey to the Society before an evening meal, and the best of the day gone out of them. And one and all have other duties, prior responsibilities, karmic links and fetters to be patiently worn through. Yet these are the people to whom I wrote those letters in reply to theirs; these are the writers of the answers that I have collated briefly in my chapter on Experiments in Zen. Are we to disband and wait for help from Japan, or the fares to go to Japan, or for Eastern clothing for our vigorous Western minds?

It may be that the problem largely turns on what we mean by *satori*, the goal of Zen endeavour. Is this beyond the range of previous Western mystical experience? Or did Eckhart, to name but one of Europe's greatest minds, achieve the same experience, though expressing, or attempting to express it afterwards, in very different terms? Surely there are degrees of super-rational intuitive experience. The perpetual argument between the 'Gradual' and the 'Sudden' schools of Chinese Zen has never impressed me as having real validity. The approach to any achievement, whether climbing Everest or driving consciousness through thought to No-thought, must be gradual, in the literal sense that it proceeds by steps. But the actual achievement must obviously be 'sudden', in the sense of whole and complete and, in the case of *satori*, divorced in very nature from all that went before. Either one has satori, in the sense that it is the experience of the Absolute, or one has merely achieved some other of the hundred mystical conditions of awareness of which the great minds of the world have written for so long. But in the process of approach there are flashes of the Light, glimpses of the Self-lessness which is the hall-mark of success, 'moments' which no watch can measure, in which there is knowledge but none to know.

If this be so, that there is a long path of training in preparation for the genuine experience, then the practice of those who have attempted to find and tread, and even to indicate to others such a way, is worth collating, and worth consideration. To describe this course of training is beyond the scope of the present volume, though the way it works should be clear to some extent from the letters already quoted. These at least are steps upon that way, as applied to the Western mind.

1. First, the ground must be cleared of a large accumulation of acquired and inherited wrong belief and wrong mental habits and proclivities. So important is this that it has been said that it is all that is needed. We know that in one sense we are already in *satori*, and it is only our foolish ideas, the product of ignorance, that prevent our being what we are. But in the West it is necessary, for example, to face and remove the personal God-concept and all that it implies of 'salvation by faith' alone, and to withdraw the projections by which we blame someone else, look to someone else to save us from our sins, and lean on someone else, in every situation every moment of the day.

2. In the place of these wrong principles must be planted, and gently nurtured, right principles (*a*) of the history and traditions of Zen Buddhism and the teaching of its basic scriptures, (*b*) of

Western mystical and intuitive thought, expressed in what to us is a more native idiom, and (c) of the nature of the intuition and its exclusive power to reveal the One beyond 'the opposites' which are the province of the intellect. These three between them call for wide reading, carried out as a process of deliberate study, none the less necessary because the time will come when reading can be and will be almost given up.

3. The practice of regular periods of concentration and meditation is soon found to be necessary. In theory at least it is enough to dedicate each moment of the day to the higher forms of consciousness. In practice none achieves that habit who has not first and for a long time trained the mind into the power of concentration at will on a chosen subject, and then learnt to apply that power to rising states of mystical or spiritual awareness. In the Tao Tê Ching it is written, 'Be humble and you will remain entire,' and it is a foolish conceit to imagine that we can run before we can barely stumble.

4. If it is putting it too high to say that class-work is essential, it is found by most to be helpful, at least occasionally. Collective work gives individual encouragement for work in the days between; difficulties faced together are often solved thereby, and even as in a Zen monastery the progress of the monk is stimulated, guided and if need be checked by the Master, so we in the West can help one another on a humble scale to avoid the errors of those who have gone before.

Against this graded training is the suggestion that the achievement of *satori* is most improbable without a Roshi's aid, that it may be dangerous to try for it too strenuously without that aid, and that any achievement cannot be tested without the trained assistance of one who has not only achieved his enlightenment but been further trained to teach. This may be true, but what is the alternative? The answer may lie in the story of the pupil who sat cross-legged meditating all day long.[1]

'What seekest thou here thus sitting cross-legged?'
'My desire is to become a Buddha.'
The master took up a piece of brick and began to polish it hard on a stone nearby.

[1] From Dr Suzuki's *Essays in Zen Buddhism*, III, p. 222.

'What workest thou on so, my master?' asked the pupil, Baso.
'I am trying to turn this into a mirror.'
'No amount of polishing will make a mirror of the brick.'
'If so, no amount of sitting cross-legged will make of thee a Buddha,' said the master.
'What shall I have to do, then?'
'It is like driving a cart; when it moveth not, wilt thou whip the cart or the ox?'

We shall not in the West achieve *satori* by sitting still, cross-legged or otherwise, but by fierce endeavour and strong strife. We must clear the ground, build our edifice of the intellect and then—(at least be prepared to)—jump. If we need some help for the jumping we can ask for it when we have cleared the ground and erected a mighty tower of strong and accurate thinking.

From this results will come. We shall not seek for them, for to seek with a self is to drive them further away. But they do come, in increased intuitive development, withdrawn projections, greater serenity, ability to cope with situations great and small, and the awakening of compassion which but slept before. All who have made this experiment in the last few years have changed remarkably, passing of course through periods of depression and doubt, but finding these well suffered as the price of wider awareness, deeper understanding of eternal truths, and many a brief 'experience' of things no words can usefully describe. If this be so, then even at the price of danger run, of inward agony, of weeks and months of 'the dark night of the soul,' the sun new risen is abundant recompense. Collectively yet individually, hand in hand yet marching on our own two feet, we have moved upon our way. Whither? Would Benoit say we moved but in the circle of relativity, and nowhere nearer to the Real? Is our friend in France right that all our efforts may make us a Saint but never a Sage? The answer is in the experience.

PROPHECY

Viewed from the West, Zen is the One creative Life in a new form, with a new way to it. As such it will, I think, pass through stages which we shall watch but not be able to control. It will become better and better known. But as it becomes more popular, and the quantity of literature increases, the quality will steadily deteriorate. It will be degraded and indeed prostituted to utterly unworthy ends. But before this process is far gone there will be a reaction at top levels, and more and more first class minds will take up its study seriously. As these minds will come from many fields of thought the spirit of Zen will affect them severally, invading religion, science, philosophy, psychology, mysticism and art. It will appear in new names, and be none the worse for the change. It will produce its minor masters, some genuine and some the reverse.

It will prove destructive of much dogma and of the limitations of purely conceptual thought. It will prove constructive of a new harmony between the opposites, as that of religion and science, the Self and the not-Self, of East and West. It will prove expansive of psychology and productive of a new sense of compassion. It will provide the missing quality of 'warmth' and intensive interest in the individual which the modern trends of thought and science noticeably lack.

It will appeal to the English for reasons strange to the masters of its present home. For the English are in one sense strangely mystical. They love non-sense, and their humour is based on it. If one book can epitomise this quality of the national mind it is *Alice in Wonderland*, the apotheosis of the logic of a-logic, the reign of nonsense far beyond the unkind barriers of sense. Moreover Zen works without its user having to know how. It is the last word in spiritual 'Do it Yourself.' It uses devices as needed, and all, without exception, whether scientific or 'Heath Robinson,' are happily discarded as a raft that is made but to reach the further shore. Such lavish adoption and abandonment of means must make for tolerance; for although this is a useful gadget or device for me I realise that it may not be for you, and, conversely, the Englishman is tolerant of another's ways of doing things so long as he is permitted to continue with his own.

This new release of life, of the one life bubbling up in our Western minds, will create new forms of life, *including one for Zen*. What it will be we know not, but it will not be that of the monasteries of Japan. Much will depend on the teachers and writers who pioneer the new way to satori. Where shall we get these Roshis? (But surely this is where we came in?)

Asked, 'What is Zen?' a master replied, 'Walk On!'

GEORGE ALLEN & UNWIN LTD
London: 40 Museum Street, W.C.1

Auckland: 24 Wyndham Street
Bombay: 15 Graham Road, Ballard Estate, Bombay 1
Calcutta: 17 Chittaranjan Avenue, Calcutta 13
Cape Town: 109 Long Street
Karachi: Metherson's Estate, Wood Street, Karachi 2
Mexico: Villalongin 32-10 Piso Mexico 5, D.F.
New Delhi: 13-14 Ajmeri Gate Extension, New Delhi 1
Sao Paulo: Avenida 9 de Julho 1138-Ap. 51
Singapore, South East Asia & Far East: 36c, Prinsep Street
Sydney, N.S.W.: Bradbury House, 55 York Street
Toronto: 91 Wellington Street West